THE WAYS OF LOVE

TRANSFORMING THE PERSON

A HUNDRED-DAY JOURNAL
BY STEPHEN BUJNO

En Route Books & Media, LLC
St. Louis, MO

⊛ENROUTE
Make the time

En Route Books and Media, LLC
5705 Rhodes Avenue
St. Louis, MO 63109

ISBN: 978-1-952464-37-9 and 978-1-952464-87-4
Library of Congress Control Number: 2020952123

COVER CREDIT: TJ BURDICK. COVER PHOTO BY DANTE GABRIEL ROSSETTI - SALLY LIDDELL: SOTHERBY'S ART AT AUCTION 1988-89. SOTHEBY'S PUBLICATIONS, LONDON 1989; S. 122. ISBN 0-85667-365-X., PUBLIC DOMAIN, HTTPS://COMMONS.WIKIMEDIA.ORG/W/INDEX.PHP?CURID=10496084

TO MY DEAR WONDERFUL WIFE TINA,
WHO KNOWS INTUITIVELY
WHAT FOR MYSELF HAS TAKEN BOTH DECADES AND
MULTIPLE DEGREES TO ACQUIRE, THAT IS TO UNDERSTAND
*WHAT ARE **THE WAYS OF LOVE***

Table of Contents

THEME 7: THE CHALLENGE OF SPEAKING IN A LOVING AND KIND WAY

THEME 8: THE CHALLENGE OF BEING LOVINGLY PATIENT

THEME 9: THE CHALLENGE OF LOVING GENEROSITY

THEME 10: THE CHALLENGE OF TRUST VS. ANXIETY

THEME 11: THE CHALLENGE OF SIMPLICITY OF LIFE

THEME 12: THE CHALLENGE OF LETTING GO OF ANGER FOR PEACE

THEME 13: THE CHALLENGE OF BEING COOPERATIVE VS. BOSSY

THEME 14: THE CHALLENGE OF OVERCOMING YOU WORST DEFECT

EPILOGUE

END NOTES   287

FOREWORD
DR. RONDA CHERVIN

I have been teaching courses on the nature of love and giving workshops and retreats on the same themes for some forty-five years.

About five years ago, it occurred to me that I could put together four different small books of mine about love into one volume called *The Way of Love.* The first little volume in the big book is *What is Love?* The second is called *Obstacles to Love*; the third *Making Loving Moral and Decisions* and the Fourth is *A Hundred Day Spiritual Marathon* to become a more loving person in daily life.

When I began teaching Von Hildebrand and C.S. Lewis on the Nature of Love in an M.A. program on-line for Holy Apostles College and Seminary, the students read about definitions of love in the philosophies of different philosophical masters, and also went through the Spiritual Marathon, spending 100 days meditating and working on themes about love in one's everyday life such as "cooperativeness vs. bossiness" or "patience vs. anger".

What a joy for me when I learned that one of my top graduate students, Dr. Stephen Bujno, was using this marathon in his High School classes! And, even more exciting was to be able to come on via web-ex into his classroom to interact with the students.

It soon occurred to me that many of the examples I give of love and lack of love in daily living come out of my experience as a wife, mother, and grandmother. I wished Dr. Bujno would put in his own examples as a man, husband, father and professor.

But Dr. Bujno devised something even better. In his spin-off, *Ways of Love*, he situates the attempt to grow in love into the wider context of our present-day culture and its challenges.

INTRODUCTION
STEPHEN BUJNO

T he themes of *The Ways of Love* is the *heart child* of Dr. Ronda Chervin. My 'spinoff' purposely reoriented it in two ways. First, it was adapted to further absorb the boundaries of philosophical anthropology, humanistic psychology and Christian spirituality. I also have made it more pedagogical, in the sense that each prompt offers specific questions that allow you as the reader to personally be guided through the journal's reflection questions. The journal prompts are for you, posed rhetorically in the second person singular. In other words, within each journal are questions that are being asked of *you*. Since, as Dr. Ronda stated, I have used this in the classroom, those many years of experience have been transferred into the written reflections. Please note that *The Ways of Love* is ultimately grounded in your practical observations and personal experiences. Know that if at times you feel your responses are being guided rather narrowly or at other times the prompt seems slightly vague, that is intentional. The former is based on my experience in the classroom where prodding and more specific direction is needed, and the latter is specifically where I have found that your reflection must be given room to maneuver.

This entire project is really about *you*, prompted to think clearly about who *you* are! Journeying through these reflections will be transformative, if you wish it to be. There is no magical way to force someone to be honest with him or herself. Please do not misinterpret this venture as an attempt to apply pop psychology or belong to the self-help movement. These journal prompts are intentionally designed to help you understand yourself better, and that self-understanding is transformative. They will include identifying certain inclinations you have along with those 'under the radar' personal motivations. They may even speak to some not-so-hidden shortcomings which you are already well aware of, but nonetheless have not adequately addressed. *This is therapeutical, not therapy*...you should reread that statement. Being thera-peutical yet not therapy means it will not solve issues proper to a professional, but it will offer insights into your own life to facilitate personal growth. Therapeutical means it will be helpful and guide you to discovery.

In another aspect, it will philosophically integrate various facets of your own interior personhood, such as thoughts, intentions and emotions. The journal prompts will also connect you better with the lives of others in the community of persons of those you love. In being philosophical, *The Ways of Love* will be a very reflective venture. The insights you experience will lead to a surprising awareness of how intimately connected you are with your larger family or community. The main goal in the end is to have a reflective *you* appear, not to tackle those big philosophical or existential questions of life and life's meaning.

Nonetheless, the more you are self-aware and relationally integrated into your family community, so too will you more clearly be able to ask and ponder those *big* questions of purpose and meaning. Since those *big questions* belong to the realm of philosophy, you will probably be philosophizing whether you realize it or not. It is *always* the mark of a thoughtful person to not just question; a toddler can do that. But rather the goal is to ask the right questions. In this journal, you will work through those *right* questions. You will be taking the first steps in satisfying the *wonder* of your world and find meaning in your experiences.

Finally, it's impossible to determine the particular workings of spiritual growth in anyone's life. The goal with *The Ways of Love* is to modestly facilitate personal spiritual growth by challenging you in various areas of your faith-life that have been *un*explored or simply *under*explored. This is not an endeavor in free-floating spirituality—no therapeutic deism! These reflections, as is true of all Christian spirituality, are very much grounded in historical Revelation. The 'spiritual but not religious' concept within the Christian historical framework is in fact impossible, and it is a thinly veiled unconscious attempt to remove unwanted or challenging objective moral standards.

In the end, these journals are intended to foster virtues through reflection and develop your character based on those virtues. It will not be easy; grace is essential. Just as you cannot be in relation to Christ outside of a community of His Body, neither is the grace given for personal development meant solely for *your* exclusive growth. It is to be used in and for your community. In many ways, your life's purpose is to change *your* world.

How to Change the World

What follows are some brief comments on the priority for personal spiritual growth. First, anytime someone remarks, "Things are getting bad in the world," he or she will probably follow the statement with a nodding head and the response, "And it's not getting any better." Are things worse now than they were in the past? This book won't solve that riddle, but here's a hint. Consider that most who ascribe to that notion, and who are reading this introduction, enjoy the ease of a comfortable chair, spend time in front of the television and reside in a climate-conditioned house with running water and enough food in the refrigerator to sustain themselves for some time.

That's not true for everyone, of course, and in all honesty that's not exactly what is meant by 'not getting better'. They would probably concede that comfort and technological advances have improved. But they would also quickly point out that *society,* as a whole, is morally worse. It is often said that people's priorities are out of whack, even if it's always someone else they're speaking about. The lament continues...the whole world is in chaos, people talk past each other, there's more division, the rich are getting richer, the poor are further marginalized and without any concrete solution you find yourself uttering in frustration, "Something has to be done!" Do you feel that way? Some Christians even consider this to be the 'end times'. In fact, whole cottage industries have risen out of that fear. But a sensible mind must consider that there is a single common characteristic of every one of those derelict doomsday predictions. Every single prophesy of the demise of man and his world has been utterly and desperately wrong.

About that 'not getting any better,' you should consider that there never was a Golden Age of virtue; any world history undergraduate could explain that reality. But considering the overall spiritual malaise, moral relativism, disrespect and indifference to others in the present culture, things *could* be better. So, let us equally concede that this isn't the best of times either. We do not live in a time where the triumph of personal character is held as the standard of success. So how will things get better? How will the world change?

The answer to that question, which is fixed as the heading for this section, is simply resolved in the pursuit of how *you* will change yourself. For instance, can one person fix poverty, racism or corporate corruption? Yes and no. *No* in the sense that some issues are based on what can be referred to as 'structures of sin'. Those are the result of multiple factors that have embedded themselves in society over a long period of time and are very difficult to remove. But on the other hand, *yes* in the sense that it is equally true that within the structures (faceless corporations, various economic classes, members of each culture or race, etc.), individuals exist who are capable of their own personal change. Every group or class is simply an assembly of individuals writ large.

So, the change in man's world can only ever be achieved through individual *personal* transformation. That doesn't mean others cannot inspire you or you can't prod others, but you should make certain you realize you're not capable of willing growth for others, i.e., your self-determination is non-transferable. Therefore, the single hope to change the world is to spiritually, psychologically and philosophically facilitate your own growth with earnest and vigor. Control yourself, and you won't seek to 'control others'. This book sets out to help you with that goal. Here are three supporting historical opinions worth taking into account.

In 1978, Aleksandr Solzhenitsyn delivered a commencement address to the graduating class at Harvard. Solzhenitsyn was a Russian author and dissident who knew firsthand the pressures of evil in society and the misery that ensues. He suffered the pains of imprisonment as he was forcibly exiled to the harsh Gulag labor camps for some years. His speech to the students was a treatise on his take of *what's wrong with the world*.

For him, a lack of personal courage of those in the West was at the heart of it. He even pointed out that this has specifically been the mark of decline in civilizations since ancient times. In his estimation, morality has been reduced to legality. The letter of the law determines right and wrong; what can be shown to be legal in an argument is the sole guide for one's actions and assessment of moral good and evil. In this schema, personal accountability and especially personal moral restraint have been reduced to what is or not allowed by the law. It should be obvious how that conception places personal transformation aside. Laws are called in to control morality while political avenues are used to address social ills. He was very specific to state that placing one's hope in political and social reforms in modern times comes at the expense of spiritual life, *your* spiritual life.

According to Solzhenitsyn, those factors have added to the 'cult' of material comfort. This has left man especially vulnerable, as it becomes very unlikely a person will be willing to die and risk losing that comfort. He ended his address by citing the 'turn' man presently finds himself in, as an era that will exact a spiritual upsurge into the next anthropological stage. He means that no one on earth has any other way left, but upward.[1] Things are bad, but there's hope. Do you share that opinion? Do you have hope? Well, here's another perspective.

Arthur Rackham. 1912

The early 20th century prolific writer and social critic G. K. Chesterton, whose physical presence was as large as his personality and wit, tragically remains one of the least well-known characters in modern times. His influence can hardly be measured. He was and is the king of paradox.

For example, he would quip how the young are not instructed to tell the truth, precisely because they are not taught to desire the truth. To read Chesterton is to unravel riddles. You will find his quotes at the onset of each journal theme.

It is likely you've quoted or paraphrased him without being aware of it. He was a contemporary of the likes of Helaire Belloc, Oscar Wilde, H. G. Wells and George Bernard Shaw, the latter of which he famously debated. In 1910, Chesterton published a collection of his essays in a book entitled, *What's Wrong with the World*. Is that not on point for the present discussion? His self-chosen title is to further prompt his readers to realize that the very thing *wrong* is simply one does not ask what is *right*.[2] His point is that the vices are condemned, but rarely are the virtues sought. And there is a precise lack of orientation concerning the pursuit of those virtues necessary to develop moral character.

Today, it is common to speak of this moral malaise as 'man losing his way', i.e., to opine that things are not getting any better. Chesterton would agree, but his reply was, "Man has always lost his way. He has been a tramp ever since Eden."[3] So, nothing novel is happening today in man's world that couldn't be found equally true since the dawn of creation. But if you were to ask him what marks the present period as distinct from the past, he would reply that now man is not just wandering about without a rudder, he has evidently lost his address.[4] Chesterton's point is clear. What he means is that gone is the search, lost is man's goal, no more does man desire and ask what is right, but is culturally compulsive in identifying what is wrong. Again, things are bad, but there's hope. Again, I ask you, do you share that opinion? Do you have hope?

One last historical figure to consider is the 4th century B.C. philosopher and logician of great notoriety, Aristotle. His work on ethics, and one of his most popular writings, is entitled *Nicomachean Ethics*. It aimed at expounding not on the theoretical aspects of human nature and living, but on the practical understanding of man's habits and goals. Since *The Ways of Love's* power lies in ferreting out vice and defects, and building character through virtue formation with spiritual transformation, that makes mention of his work aptly suitable.

In the second book of *Nicomachean Ethics* (in modern day they are simply called chapters), Aristotle talks of how one needs time and experience to properly develop moral virtue. An obvious, but interesting notion—*remember that philosophy deals with the obvious that rarely receives reflection*—is that for many, forming one's character usually follows the pursuit of pleasure and the avoidance of pain. He refers to pleasure as the lure to vice, drawing man to do things ignoble and sordid. People mock and belittle others for the very purpose of bringing themselves satisfaction? It's perversely ironic, but those who either through fear or lack of self-esteem degrade others, do so for some temporary solace. Isn't that what motivates the bully?

He then claims that pain on the other hand remains an obstacle to performing traits of noble and blessed character. As a motivation, it too pushes one down to vice in weakness and away from virtue, which requires above all, inner strength that does not come easy.

Think of the fear some have of being alienated from particular groups, so to 'fit in' they conform to the corrupt character of others out of weakness. Or, by contrast, they show the strength of character needed to separate from the popular crowd and stand up for the mocked or marginalized. Isn't the former what paralyzes the coward from action? Isn't the latter what we recognize as courage? These virtues, according to the ancients, were to be either remedied or instilled by education. Education was to train one's self to like and dislike proper things. Society, in general, and education, specifically, has moved far from that understanding. Today, education is a means to advance economically and its success is determined by marketable income potential. Unfortunately, few would complain that the 'way up' of personal courage is missing in education.

So, in a very real way for Aristotle, personal transformation and character development had as its goal to train one's self to resist those temptations of the *vices* that are simply based in seeking pleasure and to buttress the *virtues* that require strength and endurance. Aristotle warns that it is always harder to fight against what is more difficult.[5] Isn't that obvious? If it is, then why do not people easily recognize the frailty in choosing the *modern* way that comes more easily to our nature? Shouldn't the goal be for the *modern* person to do what is right, put in the hard effort and avoid being culled into seeking pleasure? Do you share that opinion? Do you have hope? There's a way out, and this journal plays a part in aiding you along that endeavor.

Perhaps this brief montage will help set the stage for your own personal spiritual growth that lies ahead. *The Ways of Love* is to assist you in that fight. So even if things are not the worst they can be, if it is not the end of the world, as stated, things are not as they should be. Aleksandr Solzhenitsyn is correct, morality cannot be reduced to what is legal, and one's hope for societal change will not come from political or social reforms; rather, it comes from those who muster the courage to grow 'upwards'. With G. K. Chesterton, this point is well taken. How can each person correct what is wrong in the world, until they know what should be right? That 'right' is the one thing each person should desire, rather than aimless wandering. And Aristotle is as relevant today as he was over two millennia ago. The easy way is typically not the virtuous way, and the hard way does not bring the comfort man craves.

G. K. Chesterton

The Ways of Love is about developing virtues through reflection and promoting character through those virtues. It does not promote social reform, but it builds the courage for individuals to reform themselves—anything else is an attempt to use one's power over others. This journey only identifies the wrongs of your personal world in order to ferret out the rights that should be done. It does not offer an easy, feel-good way to focus only on your pleasurable attributes; rather, it provides stimulation and insights to challenge you in developing the difficult but wonderful aspects of virtue formation.

Lastly and most importantly, do not forget the transformative facets of supernatural grace. And know that grace is not something quantifiable or even accumulative, but it is the measure of your relationship and closeness to the Trinity, to the way of Love Himself. This grace is experienced in all the transformation that lies before you in the following reflections.

Not unlike the experience with your own family, you cannot *add up* how close you are becoming to your parent, sibling or child, yet that 'closeness' is very real and personally identifiable in your heart. That will be your measure with all of your grace-filled encounters and how they are drawing you closer to imaging the God of Love. When you recognize the many weaknesses that stem from your frailty, recall St. Paul's second letter to the Corinthians, when he pleaded to have his 'thorn' removed. Christ's response to Paul is also Christ's response to you when He says, "My grace is sufficient for you, for my power is made perfect in weakness."

When your spiritual orientation seems to pull you away from the ways of love towards what appears easier...remember, "The wisdom of the world is folly with God." When you're tempted to look for blame in others or in society at large, recall Christ's admonition, "First take the log out of your own eye." If your spiritual and personal transformation seems to be a long and a difficult journey, take solace in knowing God does not reckon time as the world reckons time. You will overcome your imperfections and vice in God's time. Love knows no other way and is patient with you; be patient with yourself.

Sacred Scripture tells of an infirmed man who laid at the edge of the Pool of Bethesda for many years. Each time that an angel stirred the pool, he was not able to make it into the water to be healed on his own. It was Christ who approached him, and without entering the water, healed him. This was not the expected means to his personal transformation, his healing. He expected to enter the water to be transformed on his own. An encounter with the way of Love changed that. The verse from Scripture says that he was made well. Your journey will be the same. You may have some preconceived notions of how things will go, but allow the encounter with Christ to unfold, so that you too will be made well.

In the fourth chapter of I Peter, man is not just emboldened to know, but to understand that each person with their unique gifts must be "good stewards of God's varied grace." Stewardship carries a great responsibility, but you may be assured, "Love covers a multitude of sins." It is God's nature for you to receive His love and to have that love returned to Him by you through others without hesitation. Love takes time and again, love is patient—love has its own way—The Ways of Love!

SUGGESTED APPROACH

Because *The Ways of Love* is a series of guided reflections that are meant to transform you by identifying strengths and weaknesses in character and behavior, do not think it results in a finished *product* of yourself. Yes, you will complete *The Ways of Love*, but *you* are not finished. If that point is obvious and appears underwhelming, perhaps you are not getting use yet to considering the obvious...you will!

Transformation is about personal growth. To say something transforms gives the connation of undergoing a change from *this* to *that*. But in terms of a human person, it's best not to think of this type of growth as something completed. You do not become *that* and you are never *finished*. You will improve through incremental achievements. The colloquialism 'three steps forward, two steps back' is a fine description of how things will proceed in your journey through *The Ways of Love*. Often, clichés are commonly known because they are commonly true.

With that said, *The Ways of Love* could and should be a regular exercise; yearly, every other year, etc. It's very likely that will also seem obvious when you've completed it, let's say 'round one'. If it is true that with every incremental success there is some relapse or slide backwards, then think of those steps forward, back and forward again as the flow and ebb of waves that raise your rising tide.

As for the content of your journal being private, you would not want every heart-felt response to become fodder for public consumption. So, don't write in a way that creates some fear this journal *might be found*! These should not be recorded reflections of your secrets of things not suitable for disclosure. But be honest and don't hesitate to reveal personal things, but use reason and strike a balance. Recall that *this is not therapy*. Nor is it a chance to settle scores by writing down your angry thoughts about others. And it certainly is not a substitute for confession or counseling.

Always challenge yourself and look for the not so obvious aspects of each reflection. But always write as they relate to you in the present. As with everything, think before you write, and be certain that you don't write to impress, i.e., don't pen a journal hoping that someday it will be used in your canonization process. Just write simply and honestly...this is for you, about you!

At the heading of each reflection, there is a verse from Sacred Scripture. It was carefully considered, even if sometimes shamelessly taken out of context. Allow a moment to let it sink in...say it quietly to yourself a few times. Then, after reading each reflection prompt is the phrase, "Consider it!" *That's your queue to journal!* Then, after writing your own entry, spend some time in prayer or reflection—slowly and thoughtfully. In the quiet of your heart, be with your Creator.

It is anticipated that this journal should be a daily exercise. But life happens, so if it turns out you do only three reflections a week, that remains a fine pace. Do make a plan, be flexible, but stick to your schedule. Keep it in your desk drawer, or a sock drawer if you must, whatever level of privacy makes you feel comfortable. At the end of the 100 journals, hold onto the completed reflections for safekeeping. Over the years, you *will* look back to it in the same way you look at older photographs. This is a snapshot, but more than a photograph, it's about a three-dimensional you.

KEEP IN MIND

The Ways of Love is an adaptation of Ronda Chervin's original effort entitled *100 Ways to Love: A Spiritual Marathon*. The theme and individual reflection heading are pretty much the same. The actual content is entirely original, following Chervin's pattern but simply making the journal more analytical. You will notice how it is designed to move you beyond any considerations founded on superficial feelings or mere emotional responses. Those both often conceal more than they reveal; it does not discount the role of your passions and emotions, it simply focuses the experience.

The fact that many of the themes build off each other means some of the individual reflections may appear formulaic. For instance, in my experience some people who work through *The Ways of Love* respond that there is a sensation they've *done that already*, meaning that at times you may feel you've already written on this or that. Be assured that is a false sense. It may hint that you did not adequately consider what was *specifically* being asked in that particular reflection. So, if you begin to sense this in your journey, it is possible that you've missed the point and should probably reread *Things to Consider*. The trick is to pay attention to the tone of each theme and allow any questions embedded in the reflection prompt to guide you.

Follow the specific introductions, which are intended to set the approach. Then in each reflection without stifling the Spirit, consider the suggested prompts as *is* before spreading out horizontally and interpreting it yourself. There will certainly be times where you will be moved to adapt the introductory teaching to your personal situation and environment...and that's good. Also, the theme introductions and each of the reflection prompts are not meant to be full-blown treatises on particular topics. The amount of text it would take to honestly explore issues such as broken trust, the dynamics of family life, the connection between love and contact, or inappropriate stances of superiority, etc., would themselves take up the space of chapters in a book. Here, only enough content is provided to merely whet your appetite. Perhaps a future edition could offer further available readings and sources for those who would like a deeper investigation. But keep in mind there is a stark difference between what is necessary for personal transformation and academic work. I pray that God may quicken your mind, calm your heart and conform your will to His as you move through *The* Ways of Love! God bless you...He will!

"Physician First Heal Thyself," from Aesop's Fables

"Do you see a man who is wise in his own eyes? There is more hope for a fool than for him."
Proverbs 26:12

"Examining myself and others is the greatest good to man, and the unexamined life is not worth living."
Socrates quoted in Plato's *Apology*

"For the world is in a bad state, but everything will become still worse unless each of us does his best."
Viktor Frankl in *Man's Search for Meaning*

Gratitude is a response, not a reaction. Imagine yourself out eating with some friends, and they notice you looking over at their dessert. Seeing you obviously want to taste it, they ask if you want to try it. You stick your fork in the dessert and before it touches your lips you reply, "Oh, thanks." That 'thank you' is almost an automatic reaction. You're grateful, but your reaction was reflexive. It was only a little better than being startled and turning your heard towards a loud noise.

When someone surprises you with a gift, say tickets to a movie, or a planned trip comes together because someone chips in their car for a ride, that in immediate happiness you say, 'Thank you'? To what degree is that reply simply driven because your desires or wants became fulfilled? For example, you may be thankful for a new phone, the chances to go on vacation with a friend's family, have a reliable car of your own, get some brand-new clothes...you name it. But in all honesty, is that type of 'thank you' similar to the *reaction* a happy-faced toddler gets when given a new toy? Don't misunderstand; saying 'thank you' in those instances is good, because that's being polite. But a *response* by contrast is more thoughtful. A response connects a plan to a goal. A response is closer to you giving yourself back to the other person out of gratefulness. It is more akin to 'showing' you are thankful, than simply saying it. And it takes some time and consideration to become good at it.

The clinical psychologist and Jesuit priest, Charles M. Shelton, proposed a way to promote gratitude in one's life through what he calls the 'daily gratitude inventory'. It begins with pausing long enough to be reflective, and secondly in reviewing the events and people you've encountered throughout your day. Thirdly, he suggests you relish how in so many ways your life is truly gifted in terms of people and opportunities, etc. And, finally, you should respond to the gift given to you, by becoming a giver yourself.[6] It is this last part that separates gratitude as a response from that of an automatic reaction. That requires a plan and goal to form your heart.

These next seven reflections will hopefully give you a glimpse of how gratitude 'opens the gift' of yourself. Not just for things, but also to the people behind those things you may either have taken for granted or perhaps only realized the worth when they were gone. In every journal this theme, you should always connect your gratitude to a person. People are the aim of gratitude and love, not things. Everything you receive should magnify something natural and good within you. And any response that doesn't originate from a sincere loving act is only intended to manipulate. That's contrary to love.

In Aesop's "The Travellers and the Plane Tree," they do not recognize the generous shade the tree's many branches and full foliage provides.

This doesn't mean you should not say 'thank you' just because it is sometimes automatic...that's actually the mark of good upbringing. It just means that you need to develop some technique to always be thankful for the people behind the things given or actions done. It also means that *feeling* or *not feeling* gracious at the time is not the cue to accept or not accept something sincerely from another person. You must allow others to be givers, and steer away from a scrupulous attitude. In short, accept a favor when offered. Ungratefulness is the enemy of gratitude. Receive a reasonable gift from someone, even if they struggle financially, or have little time to offer you. Do not take away someone else's opportunity to be the *giver*. That's part of your developing a gracious attitude.

In this theme, you're going to be asked to recognize how everything in your life truly is a gift ultimately from God; even if it *arrives* through others—God made visible. You should hope to move beyond a mere reaction and towards offering gratitude as a *response* to the many blessings in your life. Of course, the biggest blessings are not *things*, and that is why gratitude is connected to love. Psalm 136:26 sings, "O give thanks to the God of heaven, for his steadfast love endures for ever." So be thankful, but to be thankful, you must first love! Love is the only proper response to the people in your life. You'll consider being thankful for these necessities of life, along with things of beauty, then those people who love or have loved you. Also, you will be asked to consider the various forms of technology you enjoy and need, then in one journal to be grateful for your very self. You will be asked to consider being thankful for even the difficult times in your life; you might find that different. The last reflection will ask you to plan an entire day of gratitude...not easy. Now on to the journals!

"Grown-up people hardly ever think of being grateful for the sun and the moon and their own souls and bodies."

G. K. Chesterton in *The Illustrated London News*, 28 December 1935

JOURNAL 1

GRATITUDE FOR NECESSITIES

"Give thanks in all circumstances" (I Thessalonians 5:18)

Things to consider: Start this journey and first journal by trying to think of something you rarely think about in your everyday life that you should be very grateful for but aren't. Here's how to do it, take a mental trip around your house. What do you see in your kitchen that you probably have taken for granted? Are there cabinets to hold dishes, a sink with water, and cans of food or boxes of cereal? When you open your refrigerator, are you able to find what you're looking for? If not, you're lucky to have so much food in the fridge. Do you throw away leftovers that got spoiled because you've forgotten about them? Have you ever thought of how grateful you should be of the fact you even have leftovers? How many TVs do you have, computers, phones, etc? How about the bathroom—is there a shower, towels, a toilet, toilet paper? If so...welcome to the group known as the privileged! You are at least in the top 20% income bracket of the world. Many people on this planet don't have any of the above luxuries. Have you even thought about them as luxuries? Do you sleep under a blanket? Do you sleep on a bed? Is there heat in your house? You get the idea...see if you can come up with your own examples of the many things in your life that you should be grateful for but haven't sufficiently thought about up until now. Consider it!

MY GRATITUDE FOR NECESSITIES

JOURNAL 2

GRATITUDE FOR BEAUTY

"My heart leaps for joy and I will give thanks..." (Psalm 28:6-7)

Things to consider: Beauty will be something brought up a few times during this *marathon*. This reflection is specifically about being thankful for the beauty in *your* world and your life. Many people have a special intuition and rightly are attracted to things beautiful. Those attractions are many times to things of man-created material beauty, such as paintings, poems and song lyrics. Other times, the attraction is to God-created beauty such as sunsets, waterfalls, the sound of rain, etc. Concerning people as beautiful, you might consider an appreciation for a pretty face, or the way the person carries themselves. But beauty in people runs deeper, of course, and here's an opportunity to move beyond that surface beauty. Have you ever thought of those marks of age on a person's face as beautiful? Does it prompt you to think of the long days they might have worked in service and love? In nature, when you look at a waterfall or sunset, does that inherent beauty spark wonder which leads to an appreciation for the Creator? Can you see how the work of an artist is a blessing where their gifts appear in creative expressions of beauty? Explore your immediate world and experience; identify some specific things and people you find beautiful. Don't hesitate to write of both man-created beauty and God-created wonders. Be sure to consider too the beauty of a person's soul. If any of those 'good souls' in your life come to mind, be thankful for them! It is all a sign of God's expressed love for you! Be sure also to reflect on how His beauty manifests in those things and people of your life? Consider it!

24

MY GRATITUDE FOR BEAUTY

Journal 3

Thanksgiving for Those Who Love(d) You

"How good and holy pleasant [to] dwell together in unity" (Psalm 133:1)

Things to consider: Whom would you miss if they moved to a distant place? Not to be macabre, but whom would you miss if they unfortunately passed away? Does that make being thankful for those persons easier? This is a backward mnemonic trick, and it reveals how you sometimes take those closest to you for granted. Spend a moment to bring to mind those on whom you rely for your needs, for comfort and growth both physically and emotionally. Now move beyond both family or friends, and consider those so-called strangers that brighten up your day; a waitress that made you smile, a store clerk who was patient and kind, or maybe a gentle soul that held the door for you, a friend who was especially considerate or just any person who was gentle with you during some tough situation. Do you see how you are not just *connected* to *those* people around you, but you are very inter-dependent. Ingratitude is not about independence, or *your* taking care of you. It's more about not recognizing how the solution to your desires and needs finds fulfillment within the community of people you live with and among. So many, sooo...many people love you. Take a fresh look at your family and close-knit friends. Can you now see how grateful you are for them? And, too, you shouldn't think of those who passed away as no longer loving you; you are still very connected to them and remain inter-dependent. The reality is that death does not separate us. Write how grateful, or how not grateful you have been with those who love(d) you. Consider it!

MY GRATITUDE FOR THOSE WHO LOVE(D) ME

JOURNAL 4

GRATEFULNESS FOR TECHNOLOGY

"They have all one language; and this is only the beginning" (Genesis 11:6)

Things to consider: When you think of technology, the first things that come to mind are probably electronic devices; cell phones, flat-screen TVs, laptops, etc. Those things are certainly technology, but do not forget that in its general sense, the definition of *technology* is the knowledge through reason and experiment applied to serve man practically. The ancient Greeks understood the wider notion of technology (*techne*), which meant using techniques and processes for the sake of mankind to improve his world. This would include anything from the human person, from controlling fire to the modern-day super computers; that's quite a large category. So, in this reflection, it's okay to begin by being thankful for your cell phones and other electronic devices. But then move towards things that aren't readily considered technology, like your city's water and sewer processing, or the many examples of things you use every day which are made of plastic and rubber. Aren't those necessary materials for cars and sports, and for medical equipment? Then take a moment to think how in some ways technology has been used by those in power to control other men (over-priced pharmaceuticals, for instance) or as a means of destruction (materials for theft or unjust war). How, too, has modern technology effected the environment? Isn't it something how things you are thankful for and that are good in themselves can still easily be misused or overused? Spend a moment to work through your gratefulness for the various types of technology in your life. Consider it!

MY GRATITUDE FOR TECHNOLOGY

JOURNAL 5

THANKFULNESS FOR YOURSELF

"Before I formed you in your mother's womb, I knew you" (Jeremiah 1:5)

Things to consider: This is one of those journal reflections that most people rarely consider. When was the last time you were simply thankful for who YOU are? Before you think this is about self-affirmation, perhaps you should consider when this self-thankfulness is left unexamined—it becomes the seat of many anxieties. Start with how you should be thankful for your very existence...your contingency on God affirms you need not exist, so the fact you are alive is a gift in itself. How about the attributes of your personhood? Are you thankful for the many great qualities you possess physically, psychologically, emotionally, etc? Do none come to mind? ...then think of what others compliment you about. What could be some of your many talents: a listening ear, a friendly or steady personality, a great sense of humor, or maybe a compassionate heart? Think about it. What are some of the things about you perhaps that your Mom and Dad love(d) about you? Or something your grandparents might have shared about how special you are (were) to them? Now consider physical attributes... do you have beautiful eyes? Have people commented on how nice your hair is? Interiorly, are you empathetic, do you always have a kind word for others, do you offer your time? How about the pride of your nationality or ethnicity? Spend some time reflecting on how thankful you are for YOU! Consider it!

MY GRATITUDE FOR WHO I AM

_____
_____
_____
_____
_____
_____
_____
_____
_____
_____
_____
_____
_____
_____
_____
_____
_____
_____
_____
_____
_____
_____
_____

Journal 6

Being Grateful for Difficult Times

"For men will be lovers of self, of money, proud [and] arrogant" (II Timothy 3:2)

Things to consider: Wouldn't it be nice to create exactly what type of world to live in, and to choose only those people you wish to have live in your little bubble. Wouldn't that be a paradise allowing you to live a perfect life? Can you picture it, a dream life, in a dream house, with the perfect family and perfect friends, a job or school you love with a boss or teacher you look forward to seeing each day? That's obviously fanciful, but it wouldn't be hard to be thankful for that, would it? Yet, that's not your life; it's nobody's life. Your life is full of difficulty, obstacles, illness and eventually the loss of someone you love. How do you view these 'difficult times', when your personal crosses seem more like a curse than a blessing? It appears odd, or even paradoxical, to be thankful for things you wouldn't wish on others. But it's not just a matter of learning life's lessons through tough experiences, which contribute wisdom and insight to your character. The answer is much simpler; life has meaning and anything that is part of that life also has meaning; it's just difficult to see. And since nothing of your life in this fallen world of pain and disappointment can truly be perfect for you, always remember in your adversity that you are not destined for perfection in this world, but rather in eternity. Only those who love deeply can be hurt, and nothing can be lost if it was not first given to you, for you. Consider it!

My Gratitude for Difficult Time

Journal 7

A Whole Day of Being Thankful

"Give thanks to him; bless his name." (Psalm 100:4)

Things to consider: A 'whole day' of any type of serious commitment is difficult. It's important you plan for this day, even if you need to delay the next theme for a day or two. As a matter of fact, that may be a good plan throughout the *Ways of Love*. In any case, steer away from feeling that this day will *deprive* you of something, such as when you fast or diet. Those things 'given up' are typically good things, but 'not eating meat today' or 'one day without carbs' are both negative things you disallow yourself for some future gain. Here the whole day of thankfulness is about *positively* changing your outlook and *allowing* gratefulness to alter your personhood today...and then for the future. It is meant to counter taking things for granted, or feeling entitled, etc. So, here's a suggestion for today—again, plan on tomorrow perhaps; everything you do from the time you wake up, brushing your teeth, eating lunch, talking with a friend on the phone, saying hello to people you love...think while in that moment what life would be like without the bed, without water and toothpaste, without your lunch, without your phone or friends, without someone to love. Then at that moment just smile thankfully, at least interiorly. If your day has some difficulty, and of course it will, remember that as hard as it is to accept, to live is to suffer. Be thankful, for deep love must accompany deep hurt. Consider it!

My Whole Day Of Gratitude

Theme Two: The Challenge of Speaking in a Loving and Kind Way

It's likely you don't often listen to how others hear *you*. There are times when you want to express yourself in a kind and loving way, but it comes across as cold, prideful, irritable (feel free to add to this list whatever personally annoys you). It could be when you speak that you're misunderstood and though unfortunate, it is unintentional. It's a shame, but people cannot read your heart. The problem in speaking is that you truly want your intentions to match the impression received. Think of how frustrating it feels when others misinterpret what you mean, or don't take you seriously. How many times do you just throw your hands in the air and say, "Why do I bother, just forget it, no matter what I

In Aesop's "The Wind and the Sun," it was the not the blustering blowing of the Wind, but the glorious shining of the Sun who proved the better.

36

say you take it the wrong way, I'm done talking?" It's not always a matter of being misunderstood though. In all honesty, do you sometimes have two standards depending on who you're talking to, or where you are having the conversation?

For instance, when you talk to family and friends, there's an established relationship, and you feel the other person already 'knows' you. You suspect you're allowed to talk more straight-forward and aren't too worried about the impression you leave. But, when you are in conversations with strangers outside the home, things change. You often put your best foot forward. Consciously or not, you want them to think you're polite, educated, respectful, etc. The dynamic depends on the situation.

What about speaking quickly, slowly or loudly? Do you talk rapidly when you get excited about a topic? That makes a thought hard to follow. Or, do you speak so softly the other person or people strain to keep in the conversation. Maybe you're one of those who drags out a sentence, and the other person is never certain if you're pausing or done. Do you over-share, giving too much information? This is often from people who are kind and enjoy talking to other people, or they're lonely. Are your responses terse, so that you appear to be disinterested? Why mention all this? Because they affect not just the perception you leave, but how well your message and thoughts are understood. Recall this theme is about anything affecting loving and kind conversation, so it matters.

Another thing to consider is rudeness. Do you often interrupt others either because you can't wait to tell them your exciting news, or maybe you're not listening to what they're saying and you're simply waiting to make your point? Or it could just be that you are selfish, or impatient...there's a lot of reasons, but they all leave the same negative impression...that you're rude. Add pride to rudeness, and you'll begin boasting. Did you ever find yourself impulsively thinking, "Enough of my talking about myself, now you talk about me for a while?" It's tempting, and addicting, to receive accolades from others, and it's easy on the ears.

With this theme, you'll start out with observing loving and unloving conversations, how you engage those outside your home, and also when you're with family and friends. Then there will be reflections on how to avoid being rude, which includes your volume and tone, and overbearing speech. There will be one journal specifically to address boasting, and then a whole day to work on loving conversation. Heed the wisdom of St. Paul, where in his Letter to the Ephesians he states, "May you no longer be children, tossed to and fro and carried about with every wind of doctrine, by the cunning of men, by their craftiness in deceitful wiles. Rather, speaking the truth in love, we are to grow up in every way into him who is the head, into Christ." God bless!

> "It can never be anything but a quarrel; but the aim of all moral and all society is to keep it a lovers' quarrel."
>
> G. K. Chesterton in *The Pedant and the Savage*, 1910

The sea nymph Galatea was loved by the Cyclops, son of Poseidon. But she loved the young handsome shepherd Acis, who taunted the Cyclops and his songs of love for Galatea. This triangle of love turned deadly for the young lovers. The story is told in Ovid's *Metamorphoses*, Book III.

Journal 8

Observing Loving and Unloving Talk

"[Be] eager to maintain the unity of the Spirit" (Ephesians 4:3)

Things to consider: Today's journal is a sober observation of how you and others in your world speak to each other. Let's not forget that perception is key here. Since others can rarely know your intentions, they will make judgments on how *you* come across. This isn't just about being liked, but rather you want to be and to appear loving. Are you self-absorbed or worried about making your point, with little consideration to how your speech is heard? And how well can you *read* the dynamics of the group? For example, are you talking sports with people that don't really follow any team, or are you sharing your aches and pains with a person who is struggling more profoundly than you? Do you often get frustrated with others during a conversation? It could be one of you is immature, or overly concerned with trivial matters, or perhaps gossipy, or bragging about things either of you have done. How do you react to that? In love? Or maybe you or they have a serious demeanor; strength and confidence could be intimidating. Take a moment to think of your recent conversations. Evaluate them in terms of being loving or unloving. Look for examples in others and also how it appears when you are the one doing the speaking. Consider it!

My Loving and Unloving Talk

_____
_____
_____
_____
_____
_____
_____
_____
_____
_____
_____
_____
_____
_____
_____
_____
_____
_____
_____
_____
_____
_____
_____

JOURNAL 9

LOVING CONVERSATION OUTSIDE THE HOME

"A friend loves at all times" (Proverbs 17:17a)

Things to consider: This reflection is not about encounters you have with your family. And it would also be good to stretch beyond those familiar conversations you have with friends to focus here on the meetings with so-called strangers. About that word stranger, there's nothing inherently wrong with it. But what if you instead considered those whom you do not know yet, not as strangers, but as potential friends? It's not always easy, but loving conversation has much more to do with *your* attitude than with the other person. And, anyway, you should set the standard high, even if they don't. Ask yourself, do you initially greet a 'stranger' with a smile and possibly a handshake, or are you grumpy and cynical meeting them with a frown or shoulder shrug? Do you think you're there for their benefit, or only in terms of what they have to offer you? After your encounter, do you think you lifted up their spirit or encouraged them? Did you even think about that? Would you consider saying "God bless you" as you part company, or at the very least offering a positive compliment, such as "I hope you have a wonderful day." How might loving conversation allow this 'stranger' to become a potential friend? Could the other person be Jesus in distress? Do you reflect Jesus to other people that Love brings into your life? Consider it!

My Conversations Outside the Home

JOURNAL 10

CONVERSATIONS WITH FAMILY AND FRIENDS

"He who troubles his household will inherit the wind" (Proverbs 11:29)

Things to consider: There's something sadly ironic about the fact that those who are the closest hurt you most often. Of the many reasons this might be true, one may stem from how those closest to you know your trigger points. For example, if you are sensitive about talking too much, when the neighbor down the street reproaches you for that defect, you might be embarrassed or even feel convicted. But if a family member or close friend brings it up, you become defensive. You would think they're nagging you, or just looking for an opportunity to point it out...again. Another reason though, and this is more important, is that with people you are close to, any slight is interpreted as a betrayal of the loyalty and friendship between you both. With those in your inner circle, you expect more compassion than harshness, more understanding than criticism. But, on the positive note, this works in the reverse. To be complimented by family, because they know your heart best, lifts up your soul. Or to be affirmed by friends who *choose* to be in your circle is a tremendous boost asserting that conversation can be a means of expressing a deeply held sense of love by those in your life. How is it for you? Consider it!

My Conversations with Family & Friends

JOURNAL 11

TALKING TOO LOUD, SOFT, MUCH OR LITTLE

"When words are many, transgression is not lacking" (Proverbs 10:19)

Things to consider: At first glance, doesn't how loud or how much you speak seem a natural part of your character? Well, it might be, but that doesn't mean it has no effect on how love is expressed in your conversations. For instance, do you use an 'outdoor' voice when you're in the house? That can be abrasive, yet speaking 'too soft' can make others frustrated and have them mentally drift away. Talking too much may mean you have one of those 'large' personalities that dominates a conversation while other times you're just being nice and want to share your news—or maybe you're just nervous. Either way, if this is you, it will make other people look for the escape hatch during the conversation. Then, what's missing when you talk too little, or are withdrawn? Maybe the other person was looking for a kind word from you, was seeking your advice or verbal reassurance and they didn't get it. This reflection isn't about being perfect; it's just being keenly aware of what obstacles exist for speaking lovingly as you live your life alongside those God has put in your midst. Does any of this strike a chord with you? In what ways could you improve? Consider it!

MY TALKING TOO LOUD, SOFT, MUCH OR LITTLE

JOURNAL 12

AVOIDING RUDE MODES OF CONVERSATION

"Him who comes to me I will not cast out" (James 3:6)

Things to consider: Rudeness is sometimes intentional, and that behavior must be controlled. For instance, vulgar language is purposefully offensive. It doesn't matter if by habit it keeps slipping out. To hear it used so casually is irrational and especially unattractive. It points to an ill-formed character. With unintentional rudeness, a mental trick is to imagine a fictional scenario. Pretend you are speaking to a very kind elderly person, perhaps your mother or grandmother. What effort would you make to 'go out of your way' to be polite? Would you ever rush the other person along, or belittle him or her in speech? One other aspect to consider is body language. Are you standing sideways, or not looking them in the eye during a conversation? Do you remain sitting if they're standing? Work backwards—what makes you feel uncomfortable or unimportant? Avoid those habits with others. Finally, think of the times you are 'multitasking' during conversations. Do you glance at your phone, or the TV during a conversation? Who deserves your attention, a real person or an electronic device? How approachable are you? Whether it's your face buried in a magazine or phone screen, or whether you're always watching the news or have headphones on, do you make others feel that they must constantly interrupt you? How does rude conversation manifest itself in your day? Consider it!

My Avoiding Rude Modes of Conversations

_____

_____

_____

_____

_____

_____

_____

_____

_____

_____

_____

_____

_____

_____

_____

_____

_____

_____

_____

_____

_____

_____

_____

_____

JOURNAL 13

THE CHALLENGE OF AVOIDING BOASTING

"May the Lord cut off the...tongue that makes great boasts" (Psalm 12:3)

Things to consider: Do you like it when others boast? Even when the reason is about a genuine achievement? Probably not...people prefer humility to someone 'sharing' their successes? First, be certain to distinguish between boasting and proper pride. Any pride towards your *alma mater*, nationality, etc., is really based on appreciation and fondness; that's good and endearing. And it's okay also when you recognize your own accomplishments or skills. True humility is a genuine self-reflection, not the self-deprecation one usually thinks of...it's not humility to put yourself down. Humility becomes boasting when you fail to understand that any talent you have is both a gift from God *and* those who have nurtured it. Boasting points directly to you and has the effect (even desire?) of lowering those around you at the expense of lifting up your own esteem. Contrast self-esteem with self-worth. The latter is based on your dignity and particular gifts, the former on an assessment of yourself in relation to others. The former changes; the latter does not. Finally, consider now how elements of your self-worth may have helped, or can help, counter the temptation to boast in your own conversations. Consider it!

My Challenge of Avoiding Boasting

_____

_____

_____

_____

_____

_____

_____

_____

_____

_____

_____

_____

_____

_____

_____

_____

_____

_____

_____

_____

_____

_____

_____

Journal 14

Conversing Lovingly One Whole Day

"If I speak in the tongues of men and of angels, but have not love." (I Cor. 13:1)

Things to consider: Again, this journal reflection is your planning for an entire day of loving conversation. So, pick a day to work this out. If it is very early in the day, then make today that day. If not, no worries, simply record some suggestions for yourself as preparation. You can do that by going back and rereading the observations you've made on loving and unloving conversation. In light of the subsequent reflections, what further insights do you now have? Think specifically how you will address those 'strangers' in conversation...remember they're potential friends. What greeting will you have ready? What valediction? And about those you are blessed to call family, in what ways can your speech defuse misunderstandings, or better yet with sincere compliments what good can you say that you've been withholding. Think of a particular family member, or friend, and what you might share with him or her. If it applies to you, think about controlling your volume and speech rate. Specifically, find a way to avoid coming across rude. And if the last reflection on boasting is an issue for you, how can you turn the focus toward the other person? God places people alongside you; can your conversation draw them in lovingly for an entire day? Consider it!

MY WHOLE DAY CONVERSING WITH LOVE

_____

_____

_____

_____

_____

_____

_____

_____

_____

_____

_____

_____

_____

_____

_____

_____

_____

_____

_____

_____

_____

_____

_____

_____

_____

_____

THEME THREE: THE CHALLENGE OF LOVING FORGIVENESS VS. RESENTMENT

This is a tricky theme. Begin by thinking of all the wise advice about forgiveness you've probably heard over the years concerning God and man. That probably includes how important it is to not just forgive, but also to forget. That's not easy, and sometimes not even possible. If the wrong you suffered is ongoing, the memory does not arise from continued resentment but from the ever-present situation always before your eyes. You can't forget what is, in reality, a constant reminder. And if the hurt is life changing, such as a breach of trust in a marriage or other close relationship, it will take a special grace not just to reconcile, but to simply forgive. Plus, you might not have been in the best frame of mind when the incident occurred or was discovered, so your reactions, even if understandable, may have further disconnected the relationship...but *not* your ability to forgive.

Forgiveness is really about acceptance. You should expect a high standard of those in your life. But accept they're not perfect themselves; everyone carries his or her own chains whose weight is unknown to you. The English poet Alexander Pope said that "To sin is human; to forgive is divine."[7] What could that mean? Is it simply that to forgive is difficult, so only God can do it properly and

54

because you're human, partial forgiveness is to be accepted? No. It means that you are able to place aside the anger, not because you understand all men are weak (though that is certain), but because in forgiveness you have reached something that transcends the human person and you then share in and with the qualities of the Divine Persons. What's at stake with forgiving? Do you risk being taken advantage of because the other person will feel as though you'll *always* forgive them? St. Teresa of Calcutta would respond to forgive them anyway, and she's correct. You will only be bearing a burden of God. Isn't He taken advantage of on a regular basis by not just others, but also by you?

What happens, then, when you have been hurt? You have a choice to either forgive (not necessarily to forget) or to stew in resentment. What are some of the dynamics if you're a person who harbours resentment? Well, there is a bitterness that saturates your day. It could be you feel taken in as some sort of fool, thinking you should've known better. And maybe you sense others think that of you too, making you feel weak and vulnerable. And the other person might be trying to reduce your dignity (but thanks to the last theme you now know it only affects your self-esteem). Nonetheless, your pride has been hurt, and in many ways you are becoming more suspicious of those around you. But know forgiveness is a choice. You can choose to become hardened, resenting those who have hurt you, and build a wall that protects you from future incidents. Or you could find ways to accept that it isn't just forgiving which is divine. Unfortunately, along with it you will also experience the hurt that comes from loving with the heart of God.

In this theme, you will be asked to widen the scope of your forgiveness and find the strength to forgive family members and friends. Then in spite of personal experiences, choose to forgive those in authority who have erred and hurt you. You'll identify ways to reconcile your heart with peers, especially those you yourself have hurt.

Finally, rather than a whole day of forgiving others (how would that work out anyway? An apology tour?), you will be asked to do what may prove to be the hardest strain on your fortitude and understanding. You will be asked to learn to forgive yourself. You deserve the same charity and gentleness that is being asked of you to offer others in your world. Consider it!

"The Bible tells us to love our neighbors, and also to love our enemies; probably because they are generally the same people."

G. K. Chesterton in *Illustrated London News*, 1910

In Aesop's "The Eagle and the Fox," the Eagle lamented she could not avenge the Fox's evil breach of trust. When calamity fell upon the Eagles nest, all her brood became food for the Fox. It's often advisable to 'let things go'.

JOURNAL 15

WIDENING THE SCOPE OF FORGIVENESS

"If you forgive, your heavenly Father will forgive you" (Matthew. 6:14)

Things to consider: This is a reflection that really requires you to spend some time in thought prior to writing. Think quietly of those that have hurt your heart, spirit or body. You should write those names down in your journal...that's the entirety of the reflection. If you want to annotate with a brief point on each, that's up to you. Be specific with the names of those people. A suggestion is to only list the initials of all the people you can recall that you have been angry with or mad at for reasons great and small. Do not attempt to be exhaustive...remember to avoid scrupulosity. There's no reason to mention the 'little hurts' that wouldn't add up to anything significant. Find a balance. Know that it doesn't matter whether you have forgiven them or not at this point. But if you have forgiven them, place a checkmark, or better yet a cross, after their initials signaling that resentment and bitterness is dead. That's something to be very proud of, as it probably wasn't easy. Then, during the prayer for this reflection, thank God for the grace and prudence you had in those instances. Concerning those whom you have not reconciled or forgiven yet, pray for the guidance and ask the Spirit to move you away from resentment and towards forgiveness for God's sake. Consider it!

MY CHALLENGE OF WIDENING WHO I FORGIVE

_____

_____

_____

_____

_____

_____

_____

_____

_____

_____

_____

_____

_____

_____

_____

_____

_____

_____

_____

_____

_____

_____

_____

_____

JOURNAL 16

FORGIVING FAMILY MEMBERS

"Come now, let us reason together" (Isaiah 1:18)

Things to consider: You are often painfully aware of the hurt you cause to those closest to you. That's not always true from 'their' perspective, as they may not even recognize they have done something unjust or unfair to you. Sometimes, it's not just a matter of omission, but they feel vindicated in their actions and don't think there's anything to apologize for. There are those times, too, when a family member meant well, but things didn't turn out as planned, and it resulted in your being hurt. If that's the case, recall forgiveness is not a synonym for acceptance. But what if the hurt was intentional, causing a deep spiritual or psychological wound? If they sincerely ask for forgiveness and legitimately try to carry through with their promise, does that make it harder to forgive in some ways? Does it take away your love of stewing in your misery? Do you want them to experience *your* pain? It takes a great deal of fortitude, wisdom and grace to accept another's contrition when he or she is sorry, but you yourself are not over it yet. How many times have you hurt God? Do you expect Him to 'get over it'? Have you approached Him with the same expectations? He forgives you. Be like Christ! Forgive those who hurt you. Consider it!

My Challenge of Forgiving Family Members

JOURNAL 17

FORGIVING FRIENDS

"He does not retain his anger, because he delights in steadfast love." (Micah 7:18)

Things to consider: Betrayal and revenge are two aspects that appear to be strong obstacles to forgiving your friends. Betrayal can be the obvious hurt from having your trust undermined. This can range in form from an act of the other's irresponsible actions (the friend lacks an objective moral standard) to calculated treachery (they were out to get you). Although those examples follow the typical understanding of the word, there is also the betrayal that is felt when you set standards too high, and the friend simply doesn't live up to those expectations. This latter type of betrayal is only a pseudo-betrayal because it is based on your own unreasonable ideals. It carries with it the false notion that you can 'manage' other people. As for the second obstacle of revenge, there is that 'I'll get-even' attitude where you wish to inflict equal misery on the friend who wronged you. Here, you like to mete out pain and discomfort in hopes of recovering some sort of justice in the form of retribution. What's the goal there? There's a hoped-for element of 'being satisfied'. But your human nature usually demands more than the wrong received, and how do you measure that anyway? So, what are your obstacles to recovering friendship with those beside you in life? Consider it!

My Challenge of Forgiving Friends

JOURNAL 18

FORGIVING THOSE IN AUTHORITY

"Why not rather suffer wrong? Why not rather be defrauded?" (I Cor. 6:7b)

Things to consider: If you have a stringent aversion to anyone in authority, this reflection cannot address that defect. This concerns those not so subtle interactions when you or another in authority sees and treats the other as *only* beneath them. For instance, they're nothing more than an employee who works for you, a student you have to teach or a patient who should just listen. Not all relationships are democratic, but persons are to be respected as equals. All genuine *authority* is derived from God and is a yielding to Christ's guidance. The operative word there is genuine because in reality authority can be abused...as all good things can. So outside of extreme cases, those in authority deserve to be respected, and this must be done without undermining their own responsibilities. So, what should you do if you're not being treated correctly? Scripture says there are times when it is better to suffer an injustice than create a conflict that may cause wider disunity and possibly a greater evil. You aren't being called to be a scapegoat or inordinately timid. But in each and every situation, consider that reconciliation is better than vindication. Are you the kind of person who must be 'proven right'? Are you easy to work with, to ask something of? Consider it!

MY CHALLENGE OF FORGIVING THOSE IN AUTHORITY

_____

_____

_____

_____

_____

_____

_____

_____

_____

_____

_____

_____

_____

_____

_____

_____

_____

_____

_____

_____

_____

_____

_____

_____

_____

JOURNAL 19

CHALLENGE OF FORGIVING FRIENDS

"Be kind to one another, forgiving one another" (Eph. 4:32)

Things to consider: In this reflection, the focus shifts from those in authority over you to the peers on your own level. These peers are not all your *chosen* friends, even if you have a strong relationship with many of them. They are those who God has placed in your life, such as fellow students, employees, neighbors, teammates, etc. There is a strong motivation and investment in maintaining peace with your close friends because you enjoy being together. The difference with the 'other' friends is that you didn't necessarily 'choose' them. But it's important you live in harmony with them. In either case, the close proximity along with the variety of personalities and temperaments can be fertile ground for frequent hurt feelings, miscommunication, stress and even hostility. Here then is the important aspect of being a forgiving person that is often overlooked...it becomes a characteristic that defines you. You're *known* as a forgiving person, meaning you are endowed with the qualities necessary for that virtue such an understanding character, a peaceful spirit, a strong will and a sharp intellect that assesses the situation. By forgiving your peers, you develop closer ties with your neighbors, more harmony with your co-workers and foster meaningful friendships. How are you with forgiving these people? Consider it!

MY CHALLENGE OF FORGIVING FRIENDS

JOURNAL 20

FORGIVENESS FROM THOSE YOU HURT

"You hypocrite, first take the log out of your own eye" (Matt. 7:5)

Things to consider: Today you are being asked to be vulnerable. The other reflections on forgiveness thus far have placed all the power in your hands by identifying those who have hurt *you*. Forgiving family members, friends, peers and those in authority was *your* choice to forgive. Now in considering those whom *you* have hurt, there is little control over their response. Are you willing to ask for forgiveness and risk rejection? Do you fear that it will just 'bring it up again' and remind the other person(s) of what you have done? This will require a great strength of will. First, did you seek forgiveness from God? Start there; share that with them. Even though God has forgiven you, it's important to also approach the ones you've hurt. Concede that it's important for everyone that harmony returns; think of the reflections on the previous journals as to the many benefits of forgiving others. Even if you are not able to correct the situation because they are not present in your life (though if you can, you should), are you willing to accept the unknowable response? Have you told the people you've hurt you're sorry? Are you willing to allow time, and the inevitable mistrust to remain, while you regain their friendship? Seek forgiveness in their time, in God's time. In what ways can your humility tell them you love them? Consider it!

MY CHALLENGE OF FORGIVING THOSE I HURT

Journal 21

Forgiving Yourself

"You are all fair, my love: there is no flaw in you" (Song of Solomon 4:7)

Things to consider: What's the worst thing you have done? Knowing all the details, would you forgive someone else of it? Do you think God forgives you? Or are you pretending that He wants you to 'punish' yourself? Remember that forgiveness and acceptance are not synonyms. What habits or traits of your personality are you struggling with? What should you accept and what should you challenge yourself to change? To accept 'yourself' can be very healthy in terms of body shape, family difficulties, scholastic aptitude, athletic prowess and in certain personal relationships. Do you work hard to nurture maturity in those areas, or do you find yourself having your own pity party saying, "I'm not smart, pretty, handsome, strong, no one likes me, etc?" Shed self-loathing, yet work towards those challenges of growth. How about those 'bad' decisions you've made? Are you a difficult friend, (making yourself incompatible), confusing sexual intimacy with love (using the other person), lashing out at someone with verbal or physical violence rather than expressing yourself with poise and dignity? Forgiveness starts with you forgiving *you*. Accept you're not perfect. You're not God! Love that person in the mirror—he or she is sorry! Consider it!

My Challenge of Forgiving Myself

_____

_____

_____

_____

_____

_____

_____

_____

_____

_____

_____

_____

_____

_____

_____

_____

_____

_____

_____

_____

_____

_____

THEME FOUR: CHALLENGE OF APPRECIATING BEAUTY

You've just wrapped up themes on gratitude and speaking lovingly. The last theme on forgiveness was probably in many ways an important, but albeit draining theme. It certainly revealed many defects and laid the foundation for future challenges of spiritual growth. Dr. Ronda has prudently placed this theme about beauty next in order to lift one's spirit. To begin, then, try to remember the last time you said, "That was beautiful." Why was it beautiful? Perhaps it was when something surprised you with joy, like a terrific athletic feat, or a job interview that went well, or an exam you scored high on? Or maybe you were thinking of a person doing a kind act, or perhaps the memory of your mother or grandmother's gentleness? Those are certainly fine places to start, and they are indeed beautiful. But as usual this theme is going to stretch your understanding, and consequently, your appreciation of beauty in its many forms, so think divergently.

Beauty is a way of knowing. That notion may be new to you. But along with goodness and truth (often called the three transcendentals), beauty is something objective by which you make judgments. When you say *that* particular tree is beautiful, *that* color is beautiful, *she* is beautiful, *that* song is beautiful, etc., you are sharing something you *know*. You might be thinking you are only commenting on what you feel, because people differ on what is or isn't beautiful—you've heard it said 'beauty is in the eye of the beholder'. Although that's entirely true of trends, styles and one's own tastes, it's not fully true of the beauty that is intrinsic to many things. The reason is that you wouldn't have said *that* or *she* is beautiful in the first place if you were not admitting there were some standard present. For example, a newborn baby being held tenderly in their mother's arms is beautiful. It's not just because *you* think so. You are simply recognizing the beauty that's before you. Now, what can you *know* by experiencing that beauty? You would know that maternal tenderness is soothing, that a newborn is trustingly dependent on the mother's love, and so on. And we know by contrast what is ugly and violates that beauty; a child disrespecting his or her mother grinds against what's integral to this image. In fact, it presents a rejection of maternal tenderness and the love of the mother.

You see, beauty isn't only for artists, though they obviously are focusing in on what many take for granted. Artists teach you to value beauty, or at least should. And the value of art (all beauty for that matter) is that it reveals something profound. When you find yourself unable to articulate something beautiful, you might turn to a song, or a photo, or a painting that expresses the sentiment. Mere words don't suffice. Likewise, think of when you are confronted by majestic beauty. It is the experience of speechless moments. Consider the grandeur of a mountain with white caps and a halo of mist, the perfect melody of a musical score that sounds like math being sung, the playfulness of an animal's antics, the striking features of a face that tells a story, the kindness of strangers which restores your hope, the beauty of simplicity in life and living that reveals 'things' are not as important as people.

These are the reflections you will visit in this theme. There's beauty in each. You will end by considering those heroes in your life that are models of that beauty.

During this theme, ask God to place the crosses and difficulties to the side for you so that beauty can be brought forward to inspire and lift up your heart. Isn't all beauty from Him, and really pointing to Him? Isn't beauty a reflection of Him? When you see beauty, do you *see* Him? This theme will help orient your vision of beauty to the objective and only true standard, God. Consider it!

The Peacock is beautiful in appearance. Yet, the birds selected the Magpie as their regent choosing that which is practical over the superficial beauty of the splendid Peacock. There is something more deeply beautiful that lies within over any outward pretense.

"The Peacock and the Magpie"—Aesop's Fable.

"Wherever people are happy men will build beautiful things."

G. K. Chesterton in *Daily News*, 1906

JOURNAL 22

FINDING BEAUTY IN STRANGERS

"Blessed are the pure in heart, for they shall see God" (Matthew 5:5)

Things to consider: It takes a certain amount of purity of heart to discover beauty in strangers. Think of the random acts of kindness you've experienced: the thoughtful words you've heard spoken between customers at a checkout counter, the gentleness of a father playing with his daughters in the front lawn as you drive past, etc. Also consider the physical beauty of other people; carefully braided or natural curly hair, the way some walk with humility and shyness, the wonderful variety of outfits that proudly expresses varying ethnicities, people's beautiful faces, etc. Have you ever seen an elderly couple holding hands? It seems they never lost that 'teenage' love. Or think of those time-stopping images you might have witnessed of a nurse cheering up a young cancer patient in the hospital, or a spouse saying goodbye to his or her life-long love as death separates them. Think for a minute...then write about all the beauty that appears in those strangers God has placed in your life to inspire you, humble you, calm you, energize you, carry you through tough times and speak of His love for you! Why would it take a pure of heart to see God in those beautiful strangers? What has touched your heart? Consider it!

My Challenge of Finding Beauty in Strangers

JOURNAL 23

APPRECIATING BEAUTY IN ALL THE ARTS

"I will solve my riddle to the music of the lyre" (Psalm 49:4b)

Things to consider: There is a popular phrase that originated in 19th century France, *l'art pour l'art* which translates 'art for art's sake'. Metro-Goldwyn-Mayer's logo has the Latin translation of this phrase, *ars gratis artis,* above the roaring lion. It means art is only pure by serving no other function, even beauty (notice an irony placing it at the beginning of a commercial film?). But if art is nothing but for itself, how can it have itself as the goal? If that's true, then art cannot point to anything outside of itself? And if that's so, beauty cannot be a way of knowing and ultimately would cease pointing to a Creator. Could that be the intention? Ironically then art devolves into a commercial product—to be made and consumed. Think of the made-to-sell music produced for a mass-market. Does the modern artist consider what beauty can be revealed, or how it will sell? Do you support those artists who intend to express beauty in dance, song or poetry? Do eternal truths of justice, honor, equality, liberty, love, hope, strength and so on find a place in what you watch, look at or listen to? Do you 'consume' mundane art? In what ways do you appreciate creativity and beauty in all the arts? Or in what ways have you been unaware of the beauty of art in your world? Consider it!

My Challenge of Appreciating Beautiful Art

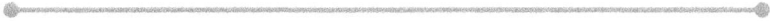

JOURNAL 24

THE BEAUTY OF LIVING SIMPLY

"The LORD preserves the simple" (Psalm 116:6a)

Things to consider: Do you equate living simply with voluntary poverty? Poverty is not the same as destitution. Destitution is sometimes referred to as abject poverty and means that you lack those things necessary for basic human needs such as adequate food, water, shelter, etc. That's not simple living. Simple living is based on the concept that all advantages of wealth, power and prestige have been given as gifts for the good of the community; they're not just for you. Consider the distinction between needs and wants. Needs include what elevates you out of destitution, but may also include luxuries such as a reliable vehicle, a dignified residence, ample leisure time, etc. But the shift in thinking comes when, once those 'needs' are satisfied, you recognize being in the realm of 'wants'. I *want* a newer car, a remodeled kitchen, a nicer vacation, a new phone, new clothing and so on. They are not 'bad' things, but could you live more simply to use God's gifts, which include earned money, to help someone else? Wouldn't that be a real example of beauty in simple living? A Redemptorist priest friend once commented on how they keep a shoebox of keepsakes; a ring their mother gave them, family photos, etc. It's thrown away when they die, as its value is only sentimental. How big would your shoebox be? How could you live simpler? What needs are really wants? How can this be beautiful? Consider it!

MY CHALLENGE OF BEAUTIFUL SIMPLE LIVING

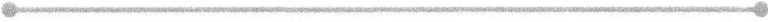

JOURNAL 25

APPRECIATING BEAUTY IN NATURE

"[Know] the wondrous works of him who is perfect in knowledge" (Job 37:16b)

Things to consider: You should find this the easiest reflection concerning beauty. Who doesn't appreciate a spectacular waterfall, or a creek winding its way through the woods, a seasonal tree blazoned in red and orange, the sun setting over the ocean, etc.? You should consider two new ways to understand the beauty that surrounds you in nature. First, begin to look for details rather than the overall view. For instance, when you see a tree covered in moss and fungus, does any 'truth' come to mind? Doesn't the growth on the tree give the impression of longevity (it's not a sapling), sharing life (the latter lives off of the former), protection (the tree shields it from the sun) and cooperation (one does not necessarily live at the expense of the other)? Secondly, in your mind, go up closer. Aren't the folds of the fungus and the softness of the moss a creation of an Artist? There's a controversy here you might not be aware of—is it beautiful because you think so, or because it is in itself? And what does that have to do with truth? C.S. Lewis' book *The Abolition of Man* says that the modern way is to say you are simply making a value statement about, for example, a waterfall, i.e., "*I* think the waterfall is sublime."[8] But Lewis contends that the waterfall is sublime in itself and that you are just discovering it. How much beauty in nature have you discovered? What truth does that beauty reveal? Consider it!

MY CHALLENGE OF FINDING BEAUTY IN NATURE

JOURNAL 26

APPRECIATING BEAUTY IN ANIMALS

"Ask the beasts, and they will teach you" (Job 12:7a)

Things to consider: Beauty in animals allows two major themes to develop. On the one hand, there is the *sheer splendor in the uniqueness* of so many species. Try to picture each animal as it is mentioned. Think of the cockatoo and the kangaroo, the whale and the jellyfish, the lion and the domestic dog. All of the variations, even within the species, simply marvel the senses. Then there are those species so unique and unfamiliar that you may have never heard of them...look them up! These animals don't even seem real, for example the sea pig, the panda ant, the mantis shrimp and the shoebill to just name a few. Sometimes, they seem like science experiments gone badly. The second theme involves the *anthropomorphic tendency* to see them possessing traits of human nature. Think of the posters or pictures you've seen of an animal with some funny text below. There is the grumpy cat with an attitude, or the squirrel in winter pleading for a morsel, or the dog whose day is so tough it can hardly stay awake. The words seem to fit the expressions. Who knows, but maybe those lines of text are what they're thinking. It may also be they possess their own beauty, and your interaction helps reveal an appreciation for a part of the wonder in them you found in yourself? How can you connect beauty to the beauty in animals? Consider it!

MY CHALLENGE OF SEEING BEAUTY IN ANIMALS

_____

_____

_____

_____

_____

_____

_____

_____

_____

_____

_____

_____

_____

_____

_____

_____

_____

_____

_____

_____

_____

_____

_____

_____

_____

JOURNAL 27

FINDING BEAUTY IN THE FACES OF OTHERS

"[Be] a person of heart with...a gentle and quiet spirit" (I Peter 3:4)

Things to consider: Dr. Ronda's daughter is a poet and spoke of her once writing in a funeral eulogy, "No one can know what it cost a person to earn his or her face." Isn't that true? Isn't the face the primary way you know a person? Neuroscience tells us that there is one thing common about beauty; it stimulates activity in the medial orbital frontal cortex. That's your pleasure center. So, you could say that beauty is something you delight in. Plato agreed and thought beauty to be the splendor of truth. But what truth could be found in another's face? What splendor may one's face reveal? Yes, the years create wrinkles, hard work will carve in lines and the sun will make soft skin tough. But even through the wrinkles, lines and rough skin one could easily recognize the 'cost' of that person's life. It may reveal the many privileged, but perhaps difficult, years and long hours each day spent in hard labor, and the exposure to the elements that came at a price of comfort, and ease of living given to family. Isn't that beautiful? Or the young girl whose face remains seraph-like, what experiences lie in wait? What future man will win that young lady's affection? What does beauty communicate? Something transcendent? In Fyodor Dostoevsky's novel *The Idiot,* the author says, "Beauty can save the world."[9] Do you find meaning in beauty? Have you found some meaning in another's face? Consider it!

My Challenge of Finding Beauty in Faces

_____
_____
_____
_____
_____
_____
_____
_____
_____
_____
_____
_____
_____
_____
_____
_____
_____
_____
_____
_____
_____
_____
_____

JOURNAL 28

BEAUTY IN YOUR HEROES AND SAINTS

"There are some standing here who will not taste death" (Mark 9:1)

Things to consider: There are *recognized* Saints, but some people also rightly admire countless others that deserve admiration. St. Francis seems to transcend those categories—of course, he is sometimes reduced to an animal lover—but nonetheless respected as kind, gentle and sincere. In ethnic households, there are typically multiple statues and icons of Saints, a Last Supper in the kitchen, various Crucifixes, a Sacred Heart of Jesus and possibly a concrete Marian shrine outside. If you have these in your home, then you understand they are *family photos*. You can always tell what's important in your life by what's hanging on the walls. How is an appreciation of the Saints and heroes in your life displayed in the rooms and shelves in your house? Is this something you're hesitant to display? Why? Think of what religious person, art or icon inspires you. Why not place a statue or icon of them in your house? The religious Saints are part of the Body of Christ; they've just gone to their union with the Trinity before you. They're not God, but they're god-like. What of other heroes from history or country, why not display them? Doesn't this exhibit your professed values? How do your 'walls speak of or demonstrate your priorities? Or don't they? Consider it!

_____

_____

_____

_____

_____

_____

_____

_____

_____

_____

_____

_____

_____

_____

_____

_____

_____

_____

_____

_____

_____

_____

_____

_____

_____

_____

THEME FIVE: LOVING WAYS TO GIVE ADVICE

The first thing to recognize with this theme is that 'loving advice' is not a synonym for 'giving instructions'. If someone is asking for your advice, they're not seeking your sage wisdom to walk them through the steps to a solution. This is not a critique of professional or expert counseling, where the dynamic of patient/client is necessary. No, the following seven reflections concern the everyday pedestrian wisdom and insight that is sought and shared between family, friends and acquaintances. With these peer-to-peer relationships, if you don't find and use loving ways to give advice, what is at stake? Many things, and chief among them is the loss of love! St. Paul said in his first letter to the Corinthians, "Love is patient and kind; love is not jealous or boastful; it is not arrogant or rude. Love does not insist on its own way; it is not irritable or resentful; it does not rejoice at wrong, but rejoices in the right. Love bears all things, believes all things, hopes all things, and endures all things." That's the standard!

Consider the strength necessary for patience, or the self-assurance needed to avoid the urge to 'tell your story' as advice. Will you be resentful if they don't follow your grand wisdom? On some level, do you take delight in their predicament or hardship? If you're not certain your advice comes from love, then do both of you a favor and simply listen; that's not a bad alternative. This *self-assessment* also inoculates you from giving advice automatically. It doesn't become something you mentally list in bullet-point form the moment someone approaches you and asks, "Can I get your opinion on something?" But in the course of the exchange, briefly question your ulterior motives as that aids in focusing on loving advice in the conversation. They did not just come to you, but they were brought to you by Christ who wants you to speak for Him: knowing that helps. The trick will be for you to begin in silence....more on that shortly.

In this theme, then, you will begin by recalling when you've observed loving and unloving advice in your life. It's always good to work from personal experiences, as they can be a fine teacher sometimes. Then consideration will be given to determining if the advice was solicited, or if you're automatically putting your two cents in. Then you will explore advice within the dynamics at school or work, and among those exchanges with close family and friends. As will be seen, the latter two are especially susceptible to manifest manipulative motives. You also will be prompted to focus on always giving gentle advice with a humble heart so as to not control others. This theme will conclude with an entire journal reflection on loving silence. That will be challenging.

You should heed Plato's famous admonition to "first know thyself." Silence helps with that; it is your preparation for future encounters. It's your training. It also refers to being silent in order to listen and deliberate prior to responding. The benefit there is to determine whether advice is even being sought, or if the other person simply needs your ear to bounce off some thoughts. And if it's support that is needed, just affirm the other people, don't make it your goal to *fix* them. You'll be asked to put yourself in their place and think how *you* would interpret the motive and support. Would you see it as giving loving advice, or the chance to feel superior? Let that be your guide. Psalm 77:6 reads, "I commune with my heart in the night; I meditate and search my spirit." A daily mantra such as that will lay the foundation. It's hard to ask for advice, so humble yourself in giving advice. Again, if you're not certain what to say, then say nothing, and in whatever way appropriate to the relationship, simply tell them you love them, or that you'll pray for them! And do it! Consider it!

There is something clearly self-defeating in not wanting another to succeed. In Aesop's Fable "The Two Enemies," one sailor took delight in seeing the other perish below the waves. The sad irony was that they were both on the same boat.

"The error is always in treating the soul as a product and never treating it as an origin."

G. K. Chesterton in *Illustrate London News*, 1924

JOURNAL 29

OBSERVING LOVING AND UNLOVING ADVICE

"Better is a poor and wise youth than an old and foolish king" (Qoh. 4:13)

Things to consider: You don't have to be a fly on the wall to observe loving and unloving advice. In any given day, you probably find yourself saying 'Thank you' to someone whom you've reached out to and were present for your need. Or you've witnessed someone giving advice that was caring, gentle or kind. And it's equally certain there were probably the same number of times you had realized the person giving advice was sarcastically mocking the other individual to make themselves feel superior; let's face it, sometimes people are just jerks. But you learn a lot by scrutinizing other's behavior and speech in observing advice. At the very least, you learn what type of advice you like to hear, and the way you like it said. The Golden Rule comes into play here. So, in your observations, did you notice if the person asked for advice first? Did the other person act like an expert? Did you notice if the people giving advice humbled themselves, or did they belittle the person? Was the advice good and solid, or did it involve a lot of speculation? Critique yourself. How do your observations contribute to the way you offer advice in your own life? Do you realize that God needs you to speak for Him sometimes? If that doesn't come to mind often, it could be humbling. Consider it!

MY CHALLENGE OF OBSERVING ADVICE

_____

_____

_____

_____

_____

_____

_____

_____

_____

_____

_____

_____

_____

_____

_____

_____

_____

_____

_____

_____

_____

_____

JOURNAL 30

NOT GIVING ADVICE AUTOMATICALLY

"Blessed are the pure in heart, for they shall see God" (Matthew 5:5)

Things to consider: Sometimes giving unsolicited advice is based on the character flaw of being slow to listen and quick to speak. At other times, a really friendly person just loves to be helpful. A darker excuse is based in those narcissists who simply love being the 'go-to' person for guidance and instruction. The first type (those quick to speak) can have varying motives. If this is you, practice the mental trick of summing up their points to demonstrate you're listening. You will have to develop some 'presence' of the situation to not appear overbearing. Think of the person who's always 'on', their desire to make you feel better may be unconditional, but the approach thwarts the medicinal advice needed. The last type, the narcissist, is simply too self-absorbed. If they're willing to offer advice, you're only on their radar because *they* need to feel important. They can seem very charismatic, and even self-confident, but it's really a mask or persona over the shallow and fragile person underneath. They will never see something from another's perspective. The point to all this is that if you're prone to give advice automatically, it's good to identify the motive. Ultimately, it's not about you and motives are mixed. Does your loving advice put the other person in front? Consider it!

MY CHALLENGE OF CONSIDERING MY ADVICE

JOURNAL 31

GIVING LOVING ADVICE AT WORK OR SCHOOL

"Avoid such godless chatter, for it will lead people to ungodliness" (II Tim. 2:16)

Things to consider: Whether you are at school or work, there's a steady relationship in place that can be affected by how and what type of advice you give. If the relationship is peer-to-peer as with students or co-workers, then advice can easily be interpreted as bossy. If there is a hierarchy in the relationship such as manager to worker, or teacher to student, then that natural authority can bleed into how the advice is interpreted and affect how it is received. So, what approach can work? Again, it's all about humility. The person in the superior role must be humble. Being the boss or teacher doesn't make one's advice superior, but it doesn't make it wrong either. The temptation to manipulate in order to get ahead at work and look cool at school is always present. At school or work, it's often hard to know who's encouraging someone with their advice or cunningly *playing* the other person to make themselves look good. And others will think that of you. To will the good of the other is one definition of love. It works here because the way around overcoming perceived bossiness, or to be tempted to manipulate, is to have your heart set only on the other person's good. Could you do that even if it comes at your own expense? By being ostracized in school or not receiving due credit at work? Love is demanding. Consider it!

My Challenge of Advice at Work or School

_____
_____
_____
_____
_____
_____
_____
_____
_____
_____
_____
_____
_____
_____
_____
_____
_____
_____
_____
_____
_____
_____
_____
_____
_____

JOURNAL 32

LOVING ADVICE FOR FAMILY AND CLOSE FRIENDS

"Let no one seek his own good, but the good of his neighbor" (I Cor. 10:24)

Things to consider: In this reflection for a new insight, when it was your opportunity to give advice, take the perspective from the *receiving* side. Accepting direction and correction from family and close friends is an opportunity for some of the most solid advice available from those who love you most dearly. The paradox is that it is also some of the hardest advice to ask for, hear and accept. Why? Are you ashamed of 'being wrong'? Are you so independent that you want to maintain the facade you could do it 'on your own'? The issue with family and friends is that they know your idiosyncrasies, they know your needs, they know your talents and abilities, they know more often than you would like to admit what is *truly* good for you. Everyone likes to captain their own ship and not be 'steered' by others. But there's a critical distinction to make in that analogy—by taking other's advice and allowing them to guide and correct you, you are not *giving* them the steering wheel. You're just allowing them to help identify the hidden rocks ahead, the rapids coming up or the low bridge fast approaching. The gift of counsel aids in steering through difficult or unsure waters; seeking it doesn't make you a passenger sitting in the back of the boat blindly relinquishing control. Do you accept loving advice from family and friends? Do you allow many 'sets of eyes' to help you navigate well, stay afloat and arrive safely? Does that make you feel weak? Consider it!

MY CHALLENGE OF ADVICE WITH FAMILY & FRIENDS

_____

_____

_____

_____

_____

_____

_____

_____

_____

_____

_____

_____

_____

_____

_____

_____

_____

_____

_____

_____

_____

_____

_____

_____

JOURNAL 33

OFFERING ADVICE IN A GENTLE WAY

"From the fruit of his words a man is satisfied with good" (Proverbs 12:14a)

Things to consider: What does it means to be gentle? You might think of being a 'gentleman' or a 'gentlewoman'. Does being gentle simply mean to be refined and considerate? The etymology of the word is significant. To be gentle meant one was well-born or noble. Gentle comes from the root *genus*; being born into and of the same clan. Today, gentle means to be moderate in one's behavior and actions, but both meanings work for today's reflection. When first giving advice, start with the notion that the other person is on your same level, of the same clan. That will avoid the extreme mindsets of thinking, "I'm better than you" or "You probably don't want to hear what I think about it." And too often the modern connotation of being gentle, meaning to be moderate and kind, is something many people find to be a weakness. Moderation is seen to lack passion and decisiveness, and kindness is seen as both timid and soft. This reflection should help you challenge those notions. There's a popular Italian phrase, *forte e gentile*. Being *strong and gentle* go together, it is to be like Christ. In what ways are you gentle, not timid or indecisive, but full of passion and strength? How do you think you might offer advice in a Christ-like, strong and gentle way? Consider it!

My Challenge of Offering Gentle Advice

JOURNAL 34

NOT CONTROLLING OTHERS THROUGH ADVICE

"Many are the plans in the mind of man" (Proverbs 19:21a)

Things to consider: One doesn't have to be a narcissist to want to control others through advice. Though it is true that control is one of the telltale signs of narcissism, it's also a way to advance the controller's own entitlement. But there is the lesser wider-spread form, where the control allows your *ego* to exert itself. It affords you an opportunity to get what you want. To ferret out that defect, first recognize that scheming has an attractive goal. Then ask yourself, are you there for others, or are they there for you? This can be minor, such as manipulating friends to go out to eat where you want, or down-right devious where you malign someone in order to control a person's reputation. There's something called the *Personalistic norm*, which means each person should not...cannot be a means to an end (your goal); rather, each person should be an end in themselves deserving of love. Yet, power is addictive and attractive, and getting someone to secretly do your bidding is habit-forming. There's a rush in thinking, "I've got them to do that!" Obviously, this could also be for their good at times, but it is still 'managing them'. Whether it's for good or ill, do you 'use' others through advice? Consider how it makes you feel. Do you understand that it reduces their dignity? It's not easy to love. Consider it!

MY CHALLENGE OF NOT CONTROLLING OTHERS

_____
_____
_____
_____
_____
_____
_____
_____
_____
_____
_____
_____
_____
_____
_____
_____
_____
_____
_____
_____
_____
_____
_____
_____
_____
_____

JOURNAL 35

THE CHALLENGE OF LOVING SILENCE

"Better is a handful of quietness than two hands full of toil" (Qoh. 4:6)

Things to consider: If you recall, the opening theme's teaching pointed out that this journal entry would be about being silent in order to listen and deliberate prior to responding by giving advice. One benefit to that approach is to determine whether advice is even being sought, or if the other person simply wants to 'borrow' your ear. If the person just wants to vent, in lieu of advice, ask them questions instead? For instance, ask how they're holding up, if they see any light ahead, or assure them you're always available with an ear and a shoulder for support. Sometimes, people just need a confidence boost and a loving friend. If it then develops into their asking for advice, it will be welcomed and you've gained some insight. Since every situation is different, perhaps share the wisdom that worked for you. Not only is that honest and humble, but it lets them know everyone is inter-dependent and everybody needs help sometimes. Finally, remember that you're giving or offering advice, not issuing orders. If they don't take your advice, then leave it. Either they don't agree, they don't see the parallel in your examples, or it simply needs to sink in for a while. They may be turning aside your advice, but they are not rejecting you. Remember St. Francis prayed, "Grant that I may seek not so much to be consoled, as to console; to be understood as to understand." How has silence helped or hindered you giving advice to others? Consider it!

My Challenge of Loving Silence

THEME SIX: THE CHALLENGE OF LOVING SACRIFICE

Sacrifice is that one element of Christianity the modern world resists more than any other. Although there was never a golden age that could be championed as the exemplary period (remember about that in the Introduction?), the current cultural ethos is one of self-indulgence and summed up in the popular colloquialism, 'you only live once'-YOLO! To not overstate the case, this isn't evidence of crass self-centeredness. People don't flat-out admit that unnecessary *things,* such a house with more bathrooms than occupants, is more important than those persons who live *in* the home. In other words, you may not hear someone say, "The world *owes* me a happy life, so I'm pursuing it at any expense." But people's actions betray them because they often are working very hard *for* the house while neglecting the people *in* the house. Aristotle said pleasure lures people to do base and unvirtuous things, and pain prohibits them from performing transcendent and virtuous actions. That's true, and modernity's equating happiness with pleasure is the mark of contemporary culture.

What does sacrifice mean then? Does Christianity wish you misery, and no happiness or pleasures beyond the bare necessities? Not exactly, but it will take some brief explaining. First off, your orientation is supernatural. You are not destined for this life. Too many Christians equate blessings with abundance and sacrifices as some form of punishment. To reorient your thinking, know that Christianity is a relationship with the Trinitarian God who unconditionally *gifts* Himself to His creation. One could very easily say that He *empties* Himself, withholding nothing. That is *sacrifice*, that is *love* and that is *gift*. Those are synonyms. Love is not just a feeling, and a gift is not something external from your personhood. They all involve an emptying. Happiness in the eyes of God is more of a fulfillment of His gift-nature, and your being made in His image fulfills your nature in sacrifice, gift and love.

Most people think of happiness not in terms of sacrificing for others, but as a subjective contentment or satisfaction brought about by pleasure. In contrast, think of a gift as something that comes from your very person, given to another. You cannot demand reciprocation, even in terms of recognition. The idea of sacrifice is then nothing short of the giving of your very self, stemming from your very nature. Your self-giving, your self-sacrificing, your loving of another can withhold nothing. Again, should you experience no pleasures beyond the bare necessities in this life? No, but neither self-indulgence, nor YOLO fit the paradigm of gift-love-sacrifice. YOLO especially betrays your supernatural orientation. You're not meant to only live once. So, happiness is not the result of a feeling, and a life lived well may not always be pleasurable. Sacrifice always involves some action, whether it is sitting with a terminally ill loved one for hours on end, taking care of an elderly parent while putting your own plans on hold, or simply waiting patiently in line at the checkout counter because you know there are bigger issues in life.

So, in this theme you will look at sacrifice in contrast to self-centeredness. That's a good place to start. You will then reflect on how the greatest gifts are those little deeds of love. Often skipped over in sacrifice is the necessity of prayer, so you will be asked to connect the two. Then you will reflect on how sacrifice sometimes bends your will to the way of others. A small, but essential way to sacrifice is to keep your promise in a concrete way in love. Then in the final journals, you will be asked to attempt to suffer in trust, concentrating one whole day on loving sacrifice. This theme will be challenging, but fruitful. God bless! Consider it!

There is an Aesop Fable entitled "An Ass Carrying an Idol." As the Ass transported the Idol to the temple, he noticed all were bowing in reverence as he passed them by. He only later realized it was the sacred image he bore that prompted their worship.

"Every act is an act of self-sacrifice...just as when you marry one woman you give up all the others, so when you take one course of action you give up all the others."

G. K. Chesterton in *Orthodoxy*, 1908

JOURNAL 36

SACRIFICES VS. SELF-CENTEREDNESS

"He who does not love, does not know God" (I John 4:8)

Things to consider: How many times recently have you avoided doing something for another person because it was inconvenient? What reason did you use to convince yourself? Did it take much? Did you think in terms of whether it benefits *you*? That's selfishness. Maybe people around you always get what they want, and you're tired of being on the losing end of the deal? That's resentment. Or were you not going to get sufficient recognition? That's immature and narcissistic. Other reasons for self-centeredness are more nuanced; evil is subtle and cunning. Perhaps your day was guided by a sense of duty or compulsion, and any deviation would have thrown you off. Genuine responsibilities notwithstanding, how many times did other's needs prove to simply be inconvenient? Are the needs of others something that should require an appointment? Life is unpredictable, and you don't always get to choose when to sacrifice or to whom. Do you rationalize what is or is not important in your life? Do you plan who should or may have access to your time? If you're typically generous in this regard good, if not, why not? How can you sacrifice more? Consider it!

MY CHALLENGE OF SELF-CENTEREDNESS

JOURNAL 37

LITTLE DEEDS OF LOVE

"He who is faithful in very little is faithful also in much" (Luke 16:10)

Things to consider: Knowing something is true doesn't make it easy to do. Perhaps *doing* is harder than the *knowing*. Or maybe you question the veracity of the truth you claim to know. Do you think it's really true that, "He who is faithful in very little is faithful in much?" Do you really think doing little deeds leads to being trusted to do great deeds? How about testing that truth in your own life? Maybe you say "Hi" to people that look sad in order to cheer them up? That's a little deed. Could you then be trusted to give a homeless person your favorite coat? You might be questioning yourself now. If you are, okay, but you're missing the point. Being trusted to do little things doesn't mean you *will* do great deeds of love; it just means if you don't do the easy little things, it's *unlikely* you will ever do the great things. This doesn't mean that you won't be inspired at some point to do something great, but easy habits come before hard ones. So, in the end, doing little deeds of love is an indication of your character. Just as you would ask a friend who is honest in little things to hold your money, someone who finds you always doing little deeds of love will count on you in times of great need. So, how are you at doing little deeds of love? In what ways do you sacrifice? Consider it!

MY CHALLENGE OF LITTLE DEEDS OF LOVE

JOURNAL 38

SACRIFICE IN PRAYER

"In the course of time, Cain brought to the LORD an offering" (Genesis 4:3)

Things to consider: For a Christian it's common to say, "I'll pray for you" or to ask, "Will you pray for me?" It's an essential part of the Christian life and is based in the Communion of Saints. Prayer isn't unique to Christianity. Even an agnostic or atheist might say something similar by replacing 'pray' with words such as 'good thoughts'. There are two things to point out. First, you might think of prayer as something exclusively vocal, or meditative moments on your knees. That is prayer, but it would be hard to do 'without ceasing'. So how to widen your understanding of prayer? Any time you unite a gift given from God with your acceptance, that is the prayer of Blessing. When you live as though you are dependent on God, that is a form of Adoration. To ask or seek is a prayer of Petition. When you intercede for others (which must be without boundaries), that is the prayer of Supplication. To recognize all the good things God has done for you is the prayer of Thanksgiving, and finally to recognize that God is God itself is Praise. That is how to pray without ceasing. The 'obvious' second point for this journal reflection is that you are often asked to 'pray' or 'keep in your thoughts' another person or concern. How often do you really carry through with that request?—well, keeping promises as a sacrifice is only two reflections away. If you say you'll pray for someone, do so as asacrifice for them! How might you live out the other 'types' of prayer? Consider it!

My Challenge of Sacrifice in Prayer

_____
_____
_____
_____
_____
_____
_____
_____
_____
_____
_____
_____
_____
_____
_____
_____
_____
_____
_____
_____
_____
_____
_____
_____

Journal 39

Sacrificing Your Will to Others

"Present your bodies as a living sacrifice, holy and acceptable" (Romans 12:1)

Things to consider: This may be the most difficult of this theme's reflections to carry out. Think how close to your identity are the choices you make, or the decisions you arrive at. On many levels, and in many ways, to change or challenge those choices and decisions is to challenge your self-identity. In other words, to not follow your own way seems counterintuitive. There are a couple of things to consider here concerning being open to the guidance of others and suppressing (sacrificing) your own will. Firstly, there's not usually just one right way to do or think about things. So, yielding to another in this way may bring new insight, or a pleasant if even unforeseen outcome. In short, sometimes it is true that the 'more heads, the better'. Organized sports are a good method to experience the benefit of not having it 'your way'. Consider that as an example. If every 'teammate' did what he or she thought best at the time, there would be pandemonium on the field. Your not choosing the play, or getting to carry the ball, may actually produce a better outcome. With relationships, though, there is not a set goal, but it still requires practice. Start slowly by allowing a niece or nephew (or grandchild) to choose which way to go for a walk. Do you let your spouse or friend choose the movie or TV channel? These become self-teachable moments, i.e., a way for you to will 'sacrifices of love' for another. Consider it!

MY CHALLENGE OF SACRIFICING MY WILL TO OTHERS

JOURNAL 40

THE SACRIFICE OF KEEPING PROMISES

"Follow the pattern of sound words you have heard from me" (II Tim. 1:13)

Things to consider: Trust is important in all your relationships in life. There are many levels of trust, and they are usually measured by the need, severity or even urgency of the situation. So, a promise kept, broken or delayed would need to be evaluated by various factors. For instance, if you promised to remind someone to bring something to school or work and forgot, the other person may be disappointed or even upset, but it's minor and was really their responsibility to remember. Now, if someone trusted you to pick him or her up after work, and you were sidetracked or forgot, that's a different story. Not only will they assume they're low on your priority list as a friend, but there may even be safety issues depending on where they had to wait. This increases the severity. But what about promises of faithfulness, support, love and relationships? For instance, do you keep your promises when you've said, "Anytime you need me to listen to you, to support you, you can rely on my love," or "I promise to be faithful in nurturing you, upholding you and standing by you?" They don't calculate need the same way, as in promises of action. These promises, even if not severe or urgent, can deeply destroy trust if they are not kept. They are promises of your personhood. Do you promise yourself to others? Do you keep them in love and sacrifice? Consider it!

My Challenge of Keeping Promises

_____
_____
_____
_____
_____
_____
_____
_____
_____
_____
_____
_____
_____
_____
_____
_____
_____
_____
_____
_____
_____
_____
_____
_____
_____

JOURNAL 41

THE SACRIFICE OF SUFFERING WITH TRUST

"Let us not grow weary in well doing...do not lose heart" (Galatians 6:9)

Things to consider: Sacrificing is hard enough, but it seems worth it when the goal is identifiable and the steps to achieving it are clear. Athletes sacrifice by endurance and weight training, or whatever specific exercise helps develop the skills for one's particular sport. Students of all ages know that knowledge and vocational skills require a lot of sacrifice but will pay off in wisdom and achievement and the ability to support themselves, and hopefully a family. Now trust is always necessary where there is no certainty. So, the athlete must trust that his or her sacrifices will pay-off, and the student hopes his or her sacrifices will result in achievement. But what if the goal isn't so obvious or the risk is more demanding? Would you take a lower-paying vocation that is much needed and which you are well-suited for? Say, to be a social worker? What if you must sacrifice a more comfortable material life in order to live simply and use any income above your need to help the deserving less fortunate? Could you sacrifice a nicer car or fancy vacation if the reward isn't recognition, but satisfaction? Isn't this a concrete way to see if your trust is in God or money? Won't this determine if you trust in His will over your own comfort and ease? Can you trust without certainty? Consider it!

MY CHALLENGE OF SUFFERING WITH TRUST

JOURNAL 42

SACRIFICING FOR THE WHOLE DAY

"He who loves his life will lose it" (John 12:25a)

Things to consider: This is an important journal reflection on your *Ways of Love* that will require strength and planning. An entire day of sacrificing can be like saying, "Tomorrow I will begin my diet." Begin by thinking in terms of the Scripture reading. How will you lose your life today? How can you sacrifice, great or small for your family? How about friends, classmates or coworkers? What can you do to be the face of Christ for them? Then think of opportunities to help strangers. These can be by chance or a created opportunity. For example, if by chance you see that someone needs assistance, help them and make certain they feel comfortable, safe and yet independent. In terms of creating an opportunity, at home do a chore that is not ordinarily your responsibility. Or outside of the home, volunteer at a local soup kitchen, donation center, etc. And then to combine the two for an opportunity you hope presents itself, why not carry a $5 gift card with you to a local convenience store and give it to a homeless person for coffee, or even someone who seems down-on-their luck and needs a random act of kindness that day. God wants all of you...always. He wants your effort, your wealth and your time. It's a total sacrifice, and it should be all day long. These are suggestions that are corporeal works. You may also think in terms of the spiritual works of mercy. Look them up. Consider it!

MY WHOLE DAY OF SACRIFICE

Theme Seven: The Challenge of Being Friendly

It's a safe bet to say you know what friendship is. And it's fairly certain you know what it means to both be a friend and to have a friend. But it is also likely that you would have a difficult time articulating what exactly is *friendship*. You might be able to describe its characteristics, but to really get at its essence might be another matter. That's not uncommon, and it usually occurs with those things that you are most comfortable with, with those things that just seem to be essential parts of your everyday life and existence. And, ironically, it's usually the most essential yet profound aspects of one's life. So, people always start saying what a thing *is* by giving examples. You might be able to give examples of what a friend does, or list some of the characteristics surrounding the concept of friendship. You may likely conclude that it's based on some level of mutuality, a care or concern for each other, a high level of benevolence, and a shared sympathy and/or empathy. You might further recognize that friends also spend time together, consider each other when making plans, etc. These things are all certainly true. But not all friendships last do they, or stand the test of time? So, are you just more friends with some people than others, or are there distinct types of friendship?

126

In his *Nicomachean Ethics*, Aristotle famously distinguished between friendships of utility, those of pleasure and those based on the good.[10] In the case of utility, it's not mindlessly using each other, but that there is some level of mutual benefit. These are necessary in life but endure only as long as the benefit remains. Then those friendships of pleasure exist with those that you would find agreeable. Perhaps you appreciate their humor, their love of sports, etc. Both of these are genuine friendships but are only held up by changing emotions and needs. They do not last.

By contrast then, a friendship based on the good is not simply something that you have in common like hobbies or the love of a particular music genre, but a true and objective good. This is when Aristotle says you 'resemble each other in virtue'. Just as you are pleased by your own actions and enduring virtue, you will like those with whom you share those dispositions. They are known as a good. And this good is outside of each of you, such as discovering God's love, care for the poor, etc. In other words, people of like virtue share that virtue because they are pursuing a *third* good together outside of them both. And if at the end of your long life, you can count two to three in this category, you are blessed. They take so much energy, require similar strengths, sufficient opportunity and time to nurture. They are rare.

There's a saying that birds of a feather flock together. That's true for your friendships. You may not be able to choose whom you work next to, but you have total control over the company you leisurely keep. As St. Paul said in I Corinthians, "Bad company ruins good morals." With your friends, what does 'who they are' say about you? Those who are close to you, don't they share your priorities? Do they not at least in a general way speak to your own religious beliefs, your concepts of family, honor and virtue?

During this theme, you will begin by recognizing friendliness in yourself and others, and you will consider how politeness is a minimum demonstration of respect. You will examine how a loving smile is an *ah-ha* moment of the heart. You will realize the friendliness of a loving touch and that affirming others doesn't equate being in total agreement. Then there will be an opportunity to consider the importance of keeping in contact with distant friends as a loving act. You will end this theme again by looking at being friendly all day long and how that leads you closer to stepping up the ladder through the *Ways of Love*. Consider it!

THE·SICK·STAG.

In the Aesop Fable of the 'Sick Stag', many visitors came to comfort their ailing friend. All of the Stag's visitor friends ate all of his provisions; the sick Stag died of starvation, and not his illness.

"Comradeship is obvious and universal and open; but it is only one kind of affection; it has characteristics that would destroy any other kind. Anyone who has known true comradeship in a club or in a regiment, knows that it is impersonal."

G. K. Chesterton in *What's Wrong with the World*, 1910

JOURNAL 43

RECOGNIZING FRIENDLINESS

"He who walks with wise men, becomes wise" (Proverbs 13:20)

Things to consider: The great thing about the human person is that you are not a slave to your instinctual emotions. You are capable of smiling through tough times—doing so does not make you a 'fake'. Or at times it could be you have nothing emotionally left; courage is not always found in a smile. You'll have to consider these things where and when you set out to recognize friendliness in others, and possibly even within yourself. But those moments aside, what clues do you look for in other people to 'read' their friendliness? Are they smiling when they see you? Do they reach out to shake your hand or give you a hug? Do they look you in the eyes when they talk? Do they seem to be preoccupied with their phones? Do they compliment you or criticize you during the conversation? Are they engaging you while talking, or always looking for an opportunity to escape? How do you think others would respond to those questions about *you*? Some people often say, "I don't care what others think!" That might be a valid point if they're critiquing your weight, height, educational level or favorite food. But if they find you consistently abrasive, rude, egotistical, grumpy, etc., they might be forming an accurate picture of your persona, and that's not being friendly. How do you recognize friendliness in others, or in yourself? Consider it!

My Challenge of Recognizing Friendliness

Journal 44

Challenge of Being Polite

"Iron sharpens iron, and one man sharpens another" (Proverbs 27:17)

Things to consider: Politeness can vary by culture. In some cultures, polite conversation between two people is when they stand very close to one another's face. In other cultures, that invades personal comfort. Politeness can also manifest itself as an unwanted formalism. Think of the days gone by where to address someone of a higher standing without introduction would be thought impertinent. So, then, is being polite entirely culturally and period bound? Customs aside, it's based on *respect* for the person. The word comes from the Latin *re-spicere*, meaning to 'again look back'. It means to always return to basing your relationship with them on an inherent dignity and consideration as a person in their own right. So, if someone asks you a question, you answer him or her. You look at the person you are speaking to and don't talk about them in the third person while present. You should not treat those in your life as servants that must 'hold your stuff'. Respect your elders and those in authority over you. Speak to all people in your company rather than excluding or making someone feel they're 'outside'. These are all demonstrations of respect, which remains the foundation of politeness. But watch the false resemblance of politeness when it is used as a weapon or slight. To make fun of someone you think isn't pretty by politely saying, "Nice hair!" masks an insult. All good things can be twisted. Do you respect others? Are you polite? Consider it!

My Challenge of Being Polite

_____

_____

_____

_____

_____

_____

_____

_____

_____

_____

_____

_____

_____

_____

_____

_____

_____

_____

_____

_____

_____

_____

_____

_____

JOURNAL 45

CHALLENGE TO SMILE LOVINGLY

"Love one another...outdo one another in showing honor" (Romans 12:10)

Things to consider: In the past, it was thought that particular facial muscles were necessary to genuinely smile, and they created eye wrinkles. No wrinkles, no real smile; that was known as the Duchenne smile. But now it's known people could fake it rather well. This reflection is about *why* you should smile and *what* makes you smile. First, smiling is like laughing, you may have to force yourself in the beginning, but once you've begun, it gets easier and becomes contagious. Start laughing and you'll find those around you may join in. It's the same for smiling. There are biochemical explanations for those effects, of course, but even those stem from an inner joy. That's why, if it's not too much or at an improper time, most love the jokester. Everyone needs that occasional relief of built-up tension to defuse stress and strain. But the real smile comes from a realization. When you see a toddler stumbling around the kitchen, it's both comical and endearing. You realize you're catching a glimpse of carefreeness, innocence linked to physical awkwardness. It's beautiful on multiple levels. How can't that make you smile and lift up your soul? Mother Teresa always told her sisters to smile constantly. She said the beginning of love is greeting each other with a smile. Is love connected to smiling for you? Any examples? Consider it!

MY CHALLENGE OF SMILING LOVINGLY

JOURNAL 46

THE LOVING TOUCH

"One having the appearance of a man touched me, strengthened me" (Dan. 10:18)

Things to consider: There are good reasons why touch is limited. So many times, trust has been broken. But, the knee-jerk reaction of 'no contact' between nurse and patient, teacher and pupil, therapist and client is being rethought. For decades now, nurses who were in 'touch' with premature infants have seen a significant decline in mortality rates. As a matter of fact, the high mortality rate in orphanages a century or so ago has been attributed to a lack of contact, more so than malnutrition. And therapists who treat victims of sexual assault have found that 'touch' is paramount in overcoming fear and relearning trust. And teachers are often on the front-line of students struggling emotionally. Can a gentle 'touch' communicate concern and empathy? Though regulated by proper boundaries, you cannot live life in a 'glass-like' barrier. Touch communicates that the 'other' is accepted. Some of the Biblical images, and stories of the Saints who touched those who were off-limits are so moving, not because they were courageous to 'touch' someone unclean, but that their touch demonstrated acceptance of the other person. Touch broke down rejection and communicated love. Would you hold the hand of someone struggling? Put your arm around them? Isn't Christmas God 'touching' man with His Son? Consider it!

MY CHALLENGE OF TOUCHING IN A LOVING WAY

JOURNAL 47

AFFIRMING OTHERS LOVINGLY

"The companion of fools will suffer harm" (Proverbs 13:20b)

Things to consider: In Dr. Ronda's original *Way of Love: Step by Step* she noted, "A huge aspect of the Way of Love is affirming vs. criticizing others." She goes on to say, "Even if we are correct in our critical assessments, generally people need lots of affirmation in order to persevere." Think of the opportunities you had to affirm someone—did you have *their* good in mind? Criticism can be forceful, even if it's constructive. It can dash hopes and deflate one's spirit. Affirmation has that same power; it can build up dreams and prop up a tired soul. There's no harm in saying, "That is by far your best effort, good job!" or "There's no way I could have done better, you have such talent!" Even when you don't see eye to eye, affirmation can still find a way to express love. It never hurts to acknowledge effort. You could say, "I really do disagree, but I have to compliment you on thinking so thoroughly through the topic!" or "We're not going to settle this today, but you did give me a reason to sharpen my thinking on this, so thanks!" In the end, people really aren't looking for others to always agree, but they do want to be respected. That's the charm of genuine affirmation. Do you affirm others or constantly criticize them? Do you only affirm those you agree with? Do your words and actions support others or deflate them? Consider it!

My Challenge of Affirming Others

JOURNAL 48

LOVING CONTACT OVER A DISTANCE

"But there is a friend who sticks closer than a brother" (Proverbs 18:24b)

Things to consider: Technology has provided many forms of messaging and various 'video chat' options. A positive aspect of technology is that is has increased one's ability to say 'in touch' with distant friends. To send a random text is a minimal, but important way to let someone know he or she is in your thoughts. Sharing live video is really a great way to communicate the whole range of your emotions; it is the next best thing to being there. Do not discount letter writing. Putting pen to paper, placing it in an envelope and sending it off demonstrates a concerted effort. That also offers a permanence, which is missing in the electronic alternatives. But when we live in close proximity to those we love, the time and effort to keep in touch can be taken for granted, i.e., thinking they're always available. Life progresses, families move out of state, or jobs bring some to another city. School-age friends become yearbook memories, people become past neighbors, and children and parents can be pushed apart by many miles. Life is full of juggling family responsibilities, molding careers, paying the bills, fixing the car, running to doctor's appointments, etc. Those distant friendships are the first to go. How will you choose 'who' gets those precious free moments? How will you stay in loving contact over a distance of miles or time? Consider it!

MY CHALLENGE OF LOVING THOSE FAR AWAY

_____
_____
_____
_____
_____
_____
_____
_____
_____
_____
_____
_____
_____
_____
_____
_____
_____
_____
_____
_____
_____
_____
_____
_____
_____

JOURNAL 49

BEING FRIENDLY ALL DAY LONG

"A friend loves at all times" (Proverbs 17:17a)

Things to consider: You began this theme trying to recognize friendliness in yourself and others. You were asked to consider what friendliness looked like or what you considered to be friendliness. Then how being polite is minimal but necessary, and how a loving smile reflects friendliness. A little different perhaps was for you to consider a loving touch in terms of friendliness and being accepted. Speaking of acceptance, affirming others was then introduced as a way to show love and concern to those in your life. The last reflection demonstrated how keeping in contact with distant friends is an extension of love and friendliness. Now how will you plan to be friendly for an entire day? Go out of your way to smile more and leave your own comfort zone by holding someone else's hand. Can you make it a point to lift another's spirit by creatively saying something nice? Is there a family member, friend or neighbor who moved away? Reach out to them for this journal? Be specific in your responses. Remember, the goal is to express love... for just one whole day? Consider it!

My Whole Day of Being Friendly

_____
_____
_____
_____
_____
_____
_____
_____
_____
_____
_____
_____
_____
_____
_____
_____
_____
_____
_____
_____
_____
_____
_____
_____

THEME EIGHT: BEING LOVINGLY PATIENT

In this challenging theme, you will see the many consequences that follow the vice of impatience and the many benefits that accompany the virtue of patience. So, the *bads* and *goods* will settle out. Why not start with the bad, so as to end on a good note. In considering the negative effects of impatience as a weakness, here is Dr. Ronda Chervin's insight from the Danish Existentialist Søren Kierkegaard as it appeared in her original *Way of Love: Step-by-Step*.

Kierkegaard insisted that all sins come from impatience. Consider: you could be violent in action or in words because you can't stand waiting for another to obey your will. You could lie in order to get what you want rather than painfully waiting for something to happen in the right way. You could lie because you don't have the patience to convince another to forgive you, or to endure punishment and instead try to cover up your misdeeds. You could indulge in sexual sin because you don't have the trust to wait for a spouse God may send, [or grow in love and respect with your present spouse, or if you've never married to] wait for fulfillment of your greatest longings for intimacy when you can get those in a spiritual way in heaven. You rage at others because you hate what is happening, refusing to patiently accept the sufferings of your life that you cannot change or avoid.

That clearly illustrates in a few examples how impatience is at the root of your shortcomings and sins.

But there are also the positive effects of practicing patience. These are in every way a conscious choice, and achieving them requires much effort and practice. To illustrate, there was a fourth century Latin writer named Prudentius who wrote a poem entitled *Psychomachia*. The word means 'battle of souls'. In that poem, there was an epic conflict where Prudentius personified the virtues and vices (think of *Wrath* and *Patience* as people). The virtue of *Patience* was chosen to set out and destroy the vice of *Wrath* (anger). *Patience* secured peace with others. But it was through *forgiving* rather than destroying that the vice of *Wrath* didn't just yield to Patience but was driven to defeat and suicide. The moral is that given all the havoc impatience causes in one's life, patience has the capacity to overcome emotional and spiritual calamity. But it takes a great deal of courage and fortitude to be patient. In virtue theory, patience is a potential part (an auxiliary virtue) of the cardinal virtue of Fortitude. So, to be patient is to be strong. And do not forget that Fortitude is a Gift of the Holy Spirit.

Think of patience then as that capacity to accept or delay suffering and discomfort in your life. Add the grace of Christ with the power of the Spirit, and it elevates you beyond your human nature. So, over the course of the next seven reflections working toward being lovingly patient, you will begin by observing patience in yourself and others. Then, you'll reflect on how you might overcome impatience in your speech when you're frustrated. You will build and develop strength when working towards various goals in school, work and family; those are often discouragingly difficult endeavors. You'll consider especially in one reflection on how to be patient with those who express a Christian faith. And then this theme will be one that concludes with your methodically attempting to plan out twenty-four hours, or one full day of being lovingly patient. Consider it!

There was a Lion, a Bear, and a Fox. Within this fable, Aesop has the Lion and the Bear tussle over the caucus of a Fawn. The Fox, keeping her distance, simply waited until both the Lion and the Bear were too exhausted to battle each other, and also too tired to prevent the Fox from taking the fallen Fawn.

"It may be stated thus—that the more definite is our ideal the more indefinite, in the sense of infinite, must be our patience. You can define how long you will work, if you will be content with anything you can get in that time."

G. K. Chesterton in *Our Ideals and Our Patience*, 1918

JOURNAL 50

OBSERVING IMPATIENCE AND PATIENCE

"Let us run with perseverance the race that is set before us" (Hebrews 12:1b)

Things to consider: You might think you're a patient person. And you might be correct, or not! Or you might be certain you're not very patient. It's difficult to gather an honest self-assessment, so here are some question prompts to help ferret out your level of patience. Have you ever rushed someone along in their speech? Do people in front of you just not walk fast enough, or do you regularly become irritated waiting for someone to call or text you back? How about driving? Did another car go too slowly on the road, or take too long to park? The common element to all of these is the desire to force your will on another person or situation. It results in friction and disappointment. By contrast, don't you love it when someone listens to you with calmness, or a friend slows down while walking to let you catch up? A person who is patient allows others to worry about his or her own talking, walking, speaking or driving habits. Being impatient will not make people talk, walk, call back or drive faster. So, what trivial concern irritates you? Does your worrying alter anyone's behavior? How can being patient reorient your attitude? Is your impatience linked to a desire to control? Consider it!

My Challenge of Observing Patience

JOURNAL 51

IMPATIENCE IN SPEECH

"Let every man be quick to hear, slow to speak" (James 1:19b)

Things to consider: What irks you regarding speech? Do you get intimidated easily in a conversation? Are you unsure of yourself? Then focus on being a confident listener. Life isn't a game show; you can work it out and respond at another opportunity. Maybe you don't really care for the other person. Then change your goal and be magnanimous. You don't need to like everyone, but you also don't need to let those same people lead you into sin. The temptation to be rude and belittle them surfaces quickly. Maybe they have a good point you're unable or unwilling to defend and that threatens you. Concede their true point or valid argument; it doesn't mean you've lost, only that you're reasonable. Are you preoccupied with something else? The antidote then is to be in the moment, and the key is to change *your* goal. Perhaps become preoccupied with speaking to *them*, just for now. If you're tired or not feeling well at the time, it's all right to recuse yourself rather than appear unloving. Satan is a liar, and he's very good at it. He's patient only for your ruin. That's the bottom line. In the end, it is the Evil one who is provoking you to lose your patience. Remember from the initial theme's teaching that Kierkegaard regarded impatience as the basis of all sin. Know your enemy and learn the weapons that are used against you. Consider it!

My Challenge of Impatience in Speech

JOURNAL 52

IMPATIENCE WHEN FRUSTRATED

"Be not quick to anger, for anger lodges in the bosom of fools" (Qoh. 7:9)

Things to consider: It's said that frustration originates in the inability to satisfy one's needs. The first thing you must do is separate your *needs* from your *wants*. Wants aren't inherently bad, but maturity can keep them in perspective. There's a difference between needing a car to use for work and not getting to go golfing when you would like. Both might be frustrating your desires, but impatience concerning something rather trivial is juvenile and a poor reason to cause friction and irritation. But you can't downplay when there are real frustrations in life. You might feel lonely or honestly have inadequate encouragement. You may not feel well physically due to a serious illness or condition and have little support? These are real needs not being met. But just ask yourself if continual frustration improves the situation. It's easier said than done, but sometimes injustices have to be tolerated. Are there certain personalities that make your patience wear thin? Ironically, family members and close friends know best how to get under your skin. Remember Prudentius' *Psychomachia* mentioned in the theme teaching? How it meant 'battle of souls'? What was the weapon used against the vice of Anger? *Patience*! Ask yourself in what ways frustration leads to being impatient. In what ways can you react differently? Consider it!

MY CHALLENGE OF IMPATIENCE WHEN FRUSTRATED

_____

_____

_____

_____

_____

_____

_____

_____

_____

_____

_____

_____

_____

_____

_____

_____

_____

_____

_____

_____

_____

_____

_____

_____

_____

_____

Journal 53

Approaching Goals Patiently

"Seven years seemed a few days because of [his] love for her" (Genesis 29:20)

Things to consider: Have you heard the maxim, "All good things take time?" First, the goal must be 'good' or worthwhile, and, second, you should have a reasonable chance of success in achieving that goal. Consider approaching goals patiently with those two points in mind. If you neglect the first, patience is not what you require, but better discernment. If your goal is to set a record by walking backwards ten miles with your eyes closed...why? Concerning the second, if there's no foreseeable opportunity to achieve the goal, the amount of patience will have no bearing on the possibility. Not everyone will be able to play professional sports or become a professor. When it's said the goal must be good or worthwhile, that means it must not just be worthwhile to *you,* but *good* in itself. Listen to the advice of those who love you and allow them to help form your goals. That helps identify goals that are good, and not selfish. Ask in what way your goal contributes to your family, the community and your own well-being and spirituality? As for this good goal taking time, think in terms of the difference between a goal and an objective. Goals are the desired ends and objectives are the means to that goal. Objectives could be to develop study methods and to grow in wisdom while becoming a lawyer could be the goal. In what ways are your goals good? Are you patiently working towards them? Consider it!

MY CHALLENGE OF PATIENCE WITH MY GOALS

JOURNAL 54

PATIENCE IN THE FAMILY

"Here is a call for the endurance of the saints" (Revelation 14:12)

Things to consider: Being impatient with your family probably has reared its ugly head from a very young age. On long car trips, you would ask, "Are we there yet?" When you were hungry, you were told, "Wait, supper's not ready!" Christmas morning started early, and your parents likely yelled out, "Go back to bed, it's only 4:30 A.M." As you moved along in your teen years, you couldn't wait to drive, then to graduate, to get a job, to get married, to buy a house, to retire. In terms of these benchmarks, impatience arises from the conflict between your desires and your expectations. Ironically, the fact that those plateaus in life are governed by elements in society, you sometimes became more patient by necessity...everyone has to wait to be able to drive or retire. But there's another dynamic present that makes it difficult to be patient with those in your own family. They know how and when to 'push your buttons'. It hurts more deeply because you rightly expect more sympathy and love from those close to you and with relationships that are more developed. So, in what ways are you still asking, "Am I there yet?" Can you see patience with those in your family as a badge of maturity? Why are you not patient with your siblings, parents and other relatives? Consider it!

My Challenge of Patience in the Family

JOURNAL 55

PATIENCE WITH CHRISTIANS

"With all lowliness [and] patience, forbear one another in love" (Ephesians 4:2)

Things to consider: Being a Christian doesn't mean you stop being a human person. Being a Christian doesn't mean you stop being a human person. Being a Christian doesn't mean you stop being a human person. *Get the point?* If you're a Christian, you must always reflect the love of Christ. If you're a Christian, you must always reflect the love of Christ. If you're a Christian, you must always reflect the love of Christ. *Get the point?* Those two statements, quite frankly, sum up the Christian paradox. And it appears you're at a standoff. If the first statement is over-emphasized, it will be hard to distinguish you from those in the world. If it's the second statement to which you lean, you might have forgotten you're in the world. There's a famous Latin saying, *corruptio optimi pessima*, which means 'the corruption of the best is the worst'. The idea is that if those who are known to hold themselves to high standards collapse and fall from that tall perch, it doesn't get any worse. But fear shouldn't cause you to simply set the bar low, so that not only are your standards soft, but there isn't far to fall...that's digging in the ground to bury your one talent. So be patient with those attempting to climb spiritual mountains, and prop them up. Also be patient with those that are weak spiritually, and pull them up. Ask yourself how you can be more patient and less critical with Christians. Be creative. Consider it!

MY CHALLENGE OF PATIENCE WITH CHRISTIANS

JOURNAL 56

TWENTY-FOUR HOURS OF LOVING PATIENCE

"They shall run and not be weary, they shall walk and not faint" (Isaiah 40:31b)

Things to consider: This is your planning session. List specific objectives that will help you map out your whole day of being patient. Start out by being patient with yourself as the day begins. Do not set unreasonable goals. *The Ways of Love* is a growth exercise, and developing patience takes, well patience. So set a few achievable goals for patience. For instance, plan on beginning the first five minutes of your day with prayer and/or meditation. In those prayers, set targets for your patience, and ask for God's grace. You don't know you need patience until the moment it is upon you. It's likely you won't know immediately you're in a situation that requires patience. But you can plan on showing patience in specific areas of your life. Make it a point to be patient with one family member, one person at work or school, and one stranger or acquaintance. With the first two, you should name names. That's only three moments of challenge for you on this mini-marathon day of love. When the moment arrives, have a strategy to either yield for the sake of peace, remove yourself courteously from the situation, or simply try your best to understand the other person's position. Fight against anger. If you can accomplish this for just one day, and it won't be more difficult than it seems, it is an accomplishment of love for love. Consider it!

MY WHOLE DAY OF LOVING PATIENCE

THEME NINE: CHALLENGE OF LOVING GENEROSITY

This theme alongside theme eleven on "Simplicity of Life: Room for Love" are by far the ones that likely will convict you in ways you may not be comfortable with. The Catholic Church's moral teaching on life and sexuality issues appear to fall into the politically conservative camp while that same Church's revelation pertaining to the economic and social justice arena seems to belong to the liberal side. Those two facts alone should demonstrate that the Catholic Church has no comfortable home in either political ideology. But that aside, concerning loving generosity, when rightly earned monies and honestly worked for goods are acquired, it's hard for anyone to think anything else but "They're mine." Some of the following reflections will address that concept, so for now a brief statement to set the parameters will suffice. The Catholic Church is a strong proponent of property, to be cared for and cultivated in custodial fashion. It is also understood that you take better care of that which is your own. But since there is no gift in your life that originated outside of God's providence (talent, time and treasure), nothing you own could ever *just* be yours, even if it remains your choice to give away or keep. This extends even to you...*you* are not yours.

Now about those three ways you can give of yourself. Treasure, talent and time are usually referred to as the three T's. Sometimes a clear way to understand the meaning behind these words is to consider their opposites and the virtue that acts as the remedy. They will appear as *italicized* words to help. Please note that virtue theory can appear dense, so if the lingo loses you, hang on, and it will all be neatly summarized at the end.

About *treasure*: To not want to give of your own money is to be greedy. This has traditionally been known as the cardinal sin of *Avarice*, which unfortunately often presents itself as thrift or responsibly providing for an uncertain future. The antidote to Avarice is the cardinal virtue of *Temperance*. So, Temperance lines up with Treasure.

About *talent*: to refuse to extend or gift yourself is to be self-serving and is an affront to the potential part of the virtue of Justice, namely liberality. It is not, as might be your first thought, a lacking of talent but an inattentiveness to those placed in your life. It is aligned with the cardinal sin of *Gluttony*; no, it doesn't just pertain to food. So, the cardinal virtue of *Justice* is paired with exercising your Talent.

Concerning *time*: when you are tempted to busy yourself inordinately with the anxieties of life, or hoard your moments of leisure, you are being blinded to those needs of your community, family and even your own spiritual life. This could be understood broadly as falling under the cardinal sin of *Sloth*, which is a spiritual weakness where your priorities are often pushed askew. Opposed to Sloth is the cardinal virtue of *Prudence*, the *mother* of all virtues. Prudence is generally understood as right-reason applied to actions. But be forewarned, both craftiness and carnal prudence (using reason to inordinately enjoy this life) often disguise themselves as the virtue of Prudence. Satan is a liar!

Summary: In terms of *treasure*, to overcome *avarice* requires *temperance*. With your *talents*, use *justice* to overcome *gluttony*. And with using your *time*, *sloth* is undone by *prudence*.

This short treatise on those three virtues will hopefully set the stage for the following reflections. You will begin by observing generosity and stinginess wherever in life God has placed you. Then the hard topic of when and how much you are to give of your money to others will be covered. You will then look at being generous personally through your own hospitality, and how being cheerful at both school and work is a 'giving' of yourself *in* and *for* love. You will look especially as to what it means to have a heart of hospitality. Then the often overlooked, but ultimately important, role of helping those around you in little ways is an extension of generous loving. Once again, as in most other themes, you will wrap up the "Challenge of Loving Generously" by setting out a plan to extend yourself generously for one entire day. Consider it!

In Aesop's Fable of The Generous Lion, the intimidating Lion scared off the Thief who attempted to take some meat of the fallen Bullock. But a passing Traveler, recognizing the formidable beast, meekly avoided any confrontation. The Lion, being generous, called to the Traveler to come and take a reasonable share.

"But among the very rich you will never find a really generous man, even by accident. They may give their money away, but they will never give themselves away."

G. K. Chesterton in *The Miser and His Friends* 1912

165

Journal 57

Generosity and Stinginess

"One man gives freely, yet grows all the richer" (Proverbs 11:24a)

Things to consider: Typically, if asked, most people consider themselves to be fairly generous in their giving of time, talent and treasure. Your weak human nature rears its ugly head in how easy it is to see the stinginess in others while equally thinking your own generosity is obvious to all. In the modern world, there is precious little room for the three T's, and although sometimes you might go 'above and beyond,' it's probable you have some examples of how you share time, talent and treasure. Now, this is somewhat expected, as you are most aware of your own circumstances. You know what bills you have to pay, and what money comes in. You know what demands are made on your time each day, and that your talents are being used to provide for what is thought needed. But you might judge others for being lax, yet people think their giving is adequate. And they may be critical of your giving, not knowing about your life...they may even think *you're* stingy. So, the challenge with this theme is to be a better observer of generosity and stinginess within yourself. Do you have the guts for an honest solicited opinion from a friend on your giving? Pretend others are being judgmental of you, in what ways do you think they might be correct? Have you ever kept a register of your time, talent and treasure? Are the three T's used for your wants and leisure? Can you be more critical? Consider it!

My Challenge of Being Generous and Stingy

_____

_____

_____

_____

_____

_____

_____

_____

_____

_____

_____

_____

_____

_____

_____

_____

_____

_____

_____

_____

_____

_____

_____

JOURNAL 58

GIVING OTHERS YOUR MONEY

"He looked up and saw the rich putting their gifts into the treasury" (Luke 21:1)

Things to consider: "A person's superfluous income, that is, income which he does not need to sustain life fittingly and with dignity, is not left wholly to his own free determination."[11] Pope Pius XI spoke these difficult words in his 1931 encyclical *Quadragesimo anno.* So, to whose determination is it? God's! St. John Chrysostom went further, saying to deprive the poor of these goods is 'stealing'. It is true that different states in life require varied sustenance, and it is also wrong for you to give indiscriminately. You'll have to figure that out, but consider the difference between Zacchaeus, the wealthy tax collector, who climbed a tree to see Jesus, and the rich young ruler who followed all the commandments since his youth. After encountering Jesus, Zacchaeus volunteered to give half of his wealth and to return fourfold to those whom he defrauded, and then he accepted Jesus into his house. Whereas the young rich ruler, who was told he lacked one thing, was asked to sell all he had, and come follow Jesus. But he walked away sad because his possessions were many. Further, know the young rich ruler approached Jesus with the question of how one might enter eternal life. His wealth stood in the way of that salvation. Does that convict you? Ask yourself in what ways you can you live more simply for the purpose to give more generously? What do you own? What *owns* you? Consider it!

My Challenge of Giving Others My Money

JOURNAL 59

GENEROUS HOSPITALITY

"One must help the weak, remembering the words of the Lord" (Acts 20:25)

Things to consider: Hospitality is really about receiving those outside of your immediate family and relations. So, it concerns the reception of those from your larger human family into your house and heart. St. Benedict wrote, "Hospitality maintains a prominence in the living (Christian) tradition [because] the guest represents Christ and has a claim on the welcome and care of the community."[12] It's somewhat easier to invite a well-known leader from the community, a successful businessperson or a prominent politician to eat with your family. For some, this would be considered an honor. But this reflection is interested in motive. Is the person welcomed because they represent Christ? Or is it the consideration of some perceived gain, influence or notoriety that their visit brings? A traveler and beggar don't offer advantage or connections. Safety concerns aside, if it's not some random stranger but an underprivileged neighbor, would you hesitate to welcome them? And do not be tempted to think hospitality concerns only taking care of the body. It is the whole person you must welcome, providing them dignity and respect of person; this would be Christ in disguise. Do you have examples of hospitality to share? Can you reach out to anyone? Consider it!

MY CHALLENGE OF GENEROUS HOSPITABILITY

Journal 60

A Cheerful Manner at Work or School

"Bear one another's burdens, and so fulfill the law of Christ" (Galatians 6:2)

Things to consider: Have you ever thought about the fact that your cheerful demeanor at school or work is considered being generous? Remember the three T's? When you use your gift of talent (empathy, love, cheerfulness, etc.), and combine it with the willingness to give of your time, you're using two of the T's and exhibiting generosity. The trick here is to not be fooled into thinking you should only be cheerful when you're feeling content, not under pressure, perfectly healthy, and with all your relationships in good shape. That would be easy. Do you realize being cheerful is a choice? It's amazing what a smile does to someone you meet. Remember from one of the previous reflections that smiles are contagious? If your smile seems a little 'forced' in the beginning, it soon becomes quite natural, and both you and those whom you're with become enveloped in cheerfulness. It breaks down barriers, opens up opportunities, labels you as an agreeable person who's pleasant to be around. It lifts the spirit of those around you and, most of all, reflects Christ's love. So, what's the risk? The risk is you will be labeled a cheerful person. Think beyond smiles—when and how has someone lifted up your soul? Or when have you lifted up theirs? Consider it!

MY CHALLENGE OF A CHEERFUL MANNER

JOURNAL 61

HOSPITALITY OF HEART

"You shall not wrong a sojourner or oppress him" (Exodus 22:21a)

Things to consider: In the book *Living the Hospitality of God* by Fr. Lucien Richard, O.M.I., hospitality is shown to be a breaking down of barriers. It is where those 'strangers' who do not share your 'world' are brought into that affective, stable place called home.[13] It is even more intimate to allow one in the home of your heart. Fr. Richard goes on to state how this 'welcoming hospitality' is where the responsibility for each other's well-being is accepted. Each person enters into a dialogue, and the gift is a mutual transformation. You need to identify the obstacles to allowing others *in* your heart. What 'techniques' might be used to keep others in or out of your circle? Why might you want someone in or out? Do you feel superior in some way? Inferior? Do you gossip or like to 'stir the pot', pitting people against each other? Do you sit back and claim innocence? It takes real courage and trust to let others into your interior world. Strangers are people from outside your family, your social class. They are those who are not your economic equal. Think of a time when you 'missed the mark' by keeping others out. How did it disregard their well-being? And be positive, too. Perhaps you can write an example of when you showed hospitality of heart and allowed the 'stranger' into that affective, stable place of your heart where you both were transformed, and barriers between you were broken. Consider it!

MY CHALLENGE OF HOSPITALITY OF HEART

JOURNAL 62

FINDING LITTLE WAYS TO HELP

"He who sows sparingly will also reap sparingly" (II Cor. 9:6)

Things to consider: Little ways of helping don't take much of your effort or time, and they're usually free. So, why are they often rare occurrences? Because the hardest thing about helping in little ways is that they still take *some* effort and *some* time. And because they're free, you often don't think they add any significant value to your world. Here are some examples. If you see someone drop something (need help in some way), would you go out of your way to pick it up for them? How much does it cost to be friendly to the person in line next to you at the market, or when shopping? If you see someone needs affirmation, how much effort really is involved in your being kind? Are there clothes you don't wear, that don't fit or you simply don't need? Why not put them in a bag and bring them to a thrift shop? Would you wash and dry the dishes even when you didn't make them dirty? Do you speak up in defense of others? Will you take the time to become involved in a worthy cause? Besides identifying concrete examples of little ways to help, ask what occupies your time instead. Is it going to a movie or taking a walk (both good things)? Do something from your list of concrete examples to help in a small way? Consider it!

MY CHALLENGE OF FINDING LITTLE WAYS TO HELP

JOURNAL 63

CHALLENGE OF BEING GENEROUS ALL DAY

"Be rich in good deeps, liberal and generous" (I Tim. 6:18b)

Things to consider: You should be getting used to the last reflection in each theme, sometimes being a day-long attempt at putting all the previous reflections into practice. Now, go back and think about your observations on generosity and stinginess. Use those to frame the situations for your full day of generosity. You should also choose someone or some organization to donate money to that day. Choose an amount you somewhat feel uncomfortable giving away, even if you need to save up for a short while, then do that...but don't let this one slide away. Also, plan on showing hospitality to someone outside of your 'circle'...name them in your journal even if only with an initial. Here's the easy one...maybe...make it a point to be cheerful at work or school that entire day. If you have to, fake the generosity or cheerfulness...it will become natural within an hour. Then think how you can ask someone into your heart in a very different or unique way...have a plan and be creative. Finally, do something for somebody, whether they're family, friends or strangers. Make it so they cannot reciprocate. Go incognito and let God have the glory. Make your plan concrete. Put it in list form. Consider it!

MY WHOLE DAY OF BEING GENEROUS

_____

_____

_____

_____

_____

_____

_____

_____

_____

_____

_____

_____

_____

_____

_____

_____

_____

_____

_____

_____

_____

_____

_____

Theme Ten: Challenge of Trust vs. Anxiety

In cartoons long ago, and in many movies whether comedies, horror or adventure films from the 1950's through 70's, you can find various plots where characters who took one wrong step began sinking helplessly into quicksand. They were only saved if someone got there 'just in time' and could find a branch or something to hold out for them to grab. It would then be used to pull or drag them safely to the edge. It might have made some think, particularly impressionable children, that somewhere out there in the field, or lurking just behind the trees, is a deep pit of quicksand lying in wait for its next hapless victim.

Obviously, this fear wasn't rational. But did that matter? Some of your present fears are irrational, yet they still affect you emotionally, mentally and even physically all the same. And it gets worse when those many fears of yours really have a rational basis; they become a certain and distinct possibility. The cause of anxiety and worry is stress. No surprise there. But the thing to remember is that stress is caused by perception, so real or perceived; in terms of fear and anxiety, perception is reality. The truth is that whether it's real or perceived, you still must rely on someone near to reach out, or dare say pull you out to safety in your moment of anxiety, in your life's quicksand pit.

Being human is complex. You're an incarnate being. Physical injuries can affect your mental state, and one's mental anxiety can manifest itself physically. That's what makes this an important theme. In Christianity, there is no One to trust more than God, but He can't be seen except in the lives of either you or those whom you allow into your world (remember hospitality?). Without such support, anxiety can be crippling and impede your ability to manage your life effectively. The fact anxiety can be real or perceived—out there waiting in the field or lurking just behind the trees—means that having others ready there for you with a stick just in the nick of time is essential to building trust.

For the very young, trust is inherent. Babies and toddlers trust unconditionally, but they also operate at a certain level of ignorance. Once they think there's a boogeyman under their bed, it takes more than trust to convince them it's safe to go back, fearing he will grab their ankles. Why? They don't know for certain if he's gone. Now grown up, your lack of certainty with the unknown doesn't entirely go away. Because trust always retains some form of the unknown, and so does doubt for that matter, or you would simply use the word *know* to replace them both. So, what is this 'not knowing' but vulnerability, which is an inherent characteristic of trust? You don't wear armor, and life's complexities don't just 'bounce' off of you. That wouldn't require trust. Vulnerability is just one of the qualities of being a human person. And what's great about that fact is it demonstrates your interdependency with others. Maybe there really are quicksand pits in the world, but that's all right because you are not alone...ever. It's just a matter of better grasping this connectedness and identifying it as present in your relationships with others.

So, in this theme, you'll begin by observing anxiety and trust in your immediate world. Then, you will be asked if and how trust in Jesus works; all Christians say it, but what does it mean? After that, you'll be asked to place your country in God's sovereignty, and how that works. Then you will take a look at the common worries of money, school and work, along with those personal fears such as health and life. What about the Catholic Church, or Christianity in general? Are you afraid there's no faith left? And, finally, after considering those specific areas of anxiety and trust, you will again be asked to plan one whole day of trust. Consider it!

Aesop's Fable includes a notion of trust in the tale of The Bear and the Two Travelers. Upon seeing the Bear approaching, one Traveler scurries up a tree, while the other not being as quick-minded, plays dead. The bear sniffs the Traveler pretending to be dead and leaves. But while sniffing, the Bear whispered in the Traveler's ear to not trust a person who would desert a friend so easily.

"The man of the true religious tradition understands two things: liberty and obedience. The first means knowing what you want. The second means knowing what you really trust."

G. K. Chesterton in G.K.'s Weekly, 1928

JOURNAL 64

OBSERVING ANXIETY VS. TRUST

"Have no anxiety about anything...let your requests be made known" (Phil. 4:6)

Things to consider: It might be over-simplifying the point to say the unknown causes concern, and trust is linked to certainty. They're connected, but also recall that some anxiety that eats away at trust is only perceived. Don't over think this. Simply recall the times you feel or felt anxious. Think and reflect on the times you've lacked power or control. Were you overwhelmed? What overwhelms you? Whether it's work, school or your family, do you think the expectations people have of you are too high? Or too low? Is something being asked of you, but you don't have all the information to make a sound judgment? Now, reflect when you did have some power and control. Think of a time when a future desire was secure, maybe not 100%, but an alternative or fallback was available—maybe your car was acting up, but you had access to a car to borrow—was it easier to not be anxious? In what way did a support system diminish the anxiety? In what way did that leave you less vulnerable and increase the level of trust? Can you think of any circumstances that may have put your future at risk (health, home, education, etc.)? Finally, trusting in something or someone doesn't mean it will always work out the way you want. Can you think of one serious case and articulate how acceptance might be needed alongside trust? Consider it!

My Challenge of Observing Anxiety and Trust

JOURNAL 65

JESUS & YOUR AREA OF GREATEST ANXIETY

"Do not be frightened, the LORD is with you wherever you go" (Joshua 1:9)

Things to consider: Perhaps you consider yourself a Christian but have no active faith life. Maybe you are a professed and practicing Christian. Maybe sometimes you trust on your own skills, or the power of those around you when faced with great anxiety. Maybe you honestly struggle with the gift of faith and don't know what it means to trust Christ. The great thing is that Christ accepts you wherever you are. You've heard that before. But have you also heard the complete promise? He will not leave you there; that's not what love does. Consider falling alone into a deep dark hole with unsure edges—or any image of a great anxiety. If someone found you there, what would you think of them if after pulling you up, they did not offer their strength to maneuver you towards safer ground? If Christ were simply the God of faith-filled Christians, He would be a small god. Often, when life hits you between the eyes, you then admit, "I can't do it alone any more." Christ wants people to trust Him and just accept His love. Christ's love doesn't come with a condition, but it does condition you. It's Christ's strength through others, not your own, that will satisfy the greatest area of anxiety in your life right now? Do you wish to be brought up and kept on level ground by Christ? Allow others to love you in Christ, to pull you up, guiding you away from anxiety and that dark hole's edge. Consider it!

My Challenge of My Greatest Anxiety

JOURNAL 66

ENTRUSTING YOUR COUNTRY TO GOD

"All authority in heaven and on earth has been given to me" (Matt. 28:18)

Things to consider: The devoted love of one's country develops a strong passion. A country's future always holds uncertainties, and uncertainty breeds fear and anxiety. Citizens wish to preserve national identities. How many men and women have literally given their mortal lives to help build that identity? Countless others have contributed with their own time and energies in nurturing national loyalties. Anxiety at the national level differs—there's even less control and more uncertainty. The moral identity of a country could be corrected. It's just that there's so much momentum for it to turn abruptly in one's lifetime. So, any slide can have a very lasting effect for generations. Then add to that the 'wasted' efforts of all who came before you. What is one to do? Recall that Solzhenitsyn remarked that a decline in civic courage is the first symptom of the end of a country and its culture. So, begin there, be courageous! Be courageous that truth will not be suppressed, and that truth will never be annihilated. But Solzhenitsyn also said that the West puts too much hope in political and social reform. It's so hard to change a country. So, change yourself, place your country in the hands of the Source of Love. Control 'who' *you* can. In what ways can you reform yourself, for your country? Do you really trust God with your country, or politicians, judges and programs? Consider it!

My Challenge of Entrusting My Country

Journal 67

Fears About Money

"He who trusts in his riches will wither" (Proverbs 11:28a)

Things to consider: Money is a means to an end. You don't fear not having money; you fear not having money to purchase the things you want and need. And many of those are probably good things; a car, place to live, food to eat, activities with family and friends, etc. Young people worry about gas money and spending cash. Once that parental 'safety net' has been pulled away, things change. The concern is how to pay the mortgage or rent, medical bills, heat and electric, car payment(s), food, clothing, appliances, house repairs, student loans, the little things that add up (toothpaste, toilet paper, shampoo, light bulbs, mustard, napkins, towels, etc.), vacations, eating out, and so on. The good news is that people are less likely to starve to death in the developed world. Even the poor manage to 'live'. If that's you, what's the fear? A bank took a national survey (not scientific, but enlightening) and found people were more afraid of 'going broke' than dying. Why would that be? Well, your fears are tied to your desires, and if success is a large new house, sporty car and fat paycheck, losing all that makes you a failure and, apparently for some, that's worse than death. Since money is a means to an end, choose a different end. Do you choose people over things? Do you love the former and use the latter? What are your fears concerning money? Consider it!

MY CHALLENGE OF MY FEARS ABOUT MONEY

TRUSTING GOD WITH HEALTH AND LIFE

"I pray that all may go well with you and you may be in health" (3 John. 1:22)

Things to consider: When you go on vacation, you don't fear returning home. It's certain you love the carefree days and eating out, but going home isn't a *fear*. Your vacations are temporary, and *being home* is where you belong. Then why does a Christian fear death? It's said that once you have overcome the fear of death, you have it licked and can enjoy life. Once you realize this present life is not *being home,* the fear of death fades. Your health tests that logic. To hear that you should *trust* God with your health and life cannot be understood as God's keeping you in good health and endlessly preserving your life. Trust doesn't mean you get what you want. Trust has to do with being there for and with you. The parents, spouses, police and physicians you trust with your life and health have limits. They cannot fix everything. But should the God, who is able, fix everything? The world is not your home, and the redemption of suffering, including death, stands between you and your *home.* Health is a physical good. Life is the highest physical good, for without it no other goods are possible (that is the pro-life position). If you're healthy, it's so you can actively love others doing the work you were created for. Do you treat health's purpose to have as much fun in life as possible? Are you trying to get it all in before you die? Do you fear dying…living? Consider it!

MY CHALLENGE OF TRUSTING GOD WITH MY HEALTH

Journal 69

Trusting in God for the Church

"And the powers of death shall not prevail against it" (Matthew 16:18b)

Things to consider: Keep in mind trust is about 'being there' and 'being loyal' and not about things turning out *your way*. In terms of the Church, not everything that happens is God's will, but as St. Paul said in his Letter to the Romans, "In everything God works for [the] good with those who love him." Be thankful for that because the Church is made of many women and men who, even if well intentioned, are inherently flawed. And this is compounded because the Church has been around for over 2,000 years. How much evil must have people done over that length of time? That's not an excuse, but if it's true, how can one really trust the Church? Reread the title of this journal. It's trusting in *God for the Church*. That may be a distinction with little difference for many of you. Without defending any of the atrocities committed or proposing rightly so how in faith and morals the Church cannot err, consider the fact that the Catholic Church has outlived all of its enemies. It's reported that in a conversation with Pope Pius VII, the Emperor Napoleon once vowed he would destroy the Church. The Pope replied, "We the clergy have been trying to do so for 1800 years. We have not succeeded, and neither will you."[14] In what ways do you find comfort that God will 'be there' to safeguard the Church? Do you even think about that? You're part of His Body...are you helping to build or destroy? Do you trust God or man? Consider it!

MY CHALLENGE OF TRUSTING GOD FOR THE CHURCH

JOURNAL 70

A WHOLE DAY OF TRUST IN GOD

"May the God of hope fill you with all joy and peace" (Romans 15:13a)

Things to consider: By trusting God through others, it is an opportunity for God to communicate to you through them; trust builds communication skills. And trust between any two people is never isolated. It helps develop patterns of trust that affect others in your life. God is *the* example of trust, and in this trust He asks for your loyalty. His desire for your loyalty isn't the *power grab* some humans think—an opportunity for manipulating others into servitude. It's that perverted human thinking applied to God's motive that confuses so many. God's desire for loyalty is an opportunity to change your heart and mind. That's real power and one of the many fruits of trust. In the theme of teaching, it was mentioned that vulnerability is an element of anxiety and an inherent characteristic of trust. To be open to someone makes you vulnerable. So be open and make yourself vulnerable to God. Humans are driven to control you by the whims of power, fame and prestige, but can't unless you allow them. Ironically, God can control you, but he won't. Control is not a quality of love. Remember, it is only through others that His presence can be made concrete in your life. Think again about trusting God through others concerning your worries of money, your personal fears and your health and life, and your country and the Church. Be specific in your plans for this day! Consider it!

MY WHOLE DAY OF TRUSTING IN GOD

THEME ELEVEN: CHALLENGE OF SIMPLICITY OF LIFE

The Church's teaching on simplicity of life and voluntary poverty has to be the hardest to digest for most. Even the misunderstood 'sexual prohibitions' don't raise such ire as compared to the notion of the Church's 'telling' someone what they can or cannot do with *their* money. By this theme, you should be aware of how each of the gifts of your time, talent and treasure originated in God's love. They are given to you to further His kingdom by sharing them generously with those placed in your life. They funnel through you, and are not meant to increase your own power, prestige and notoriety, but reflect Christ's love.

First, there's no fine distinction between poverty and destitution. The former, even if challenging, is beneficial to one's spiritual and emotional welfare. But the second lacks a proper response to one's dignity and must be rectified. Many, if not all, are called to poverty. It is simply the state of being deficient of wants. Destitution, on the other hand, is to not have adequate food and shelter. You need to understand that clearly. It's possible you are just floating above meeting your genuine needs. It's more likely that for you and many others, poverty would be a choice.

It's important to acknowledge that most, if not all, people try to improve their economic situation. That seems natural, and if there were an opportunity for a raise, or a promotion and/or transfer that is accompanied with greater financial benefits, you would be hard-pressed to not consider it. But it's important to admit that most live larger as their means grow. The increase in income is never considered 'surplus' money. So, with greater means, you tend to proportionately raise your standard of living. You might move into a bigger house, begin to drive nicer cars, take more frequent or at least more exotic vacations, and so on. Now the response is typically, "Why not?" because the money was honestly earned. Isn't it yours to do with as you would like?

Here then is the rub. Remember, Catholic social teaching instructs that once your basic needs are met, and you are maintaining a dignified standard of living, whatever money is left over does not remain yours. For many, "*them's fightin words.*" This principle is not about paying it to the government in higher taxes, or throwing your money at inefficient or corrupt charities, or giving it to local homeless persons without discretion...though recall that destitution (lacking basic food and adequate shelter) is below one's dignity, and substance abuse and laziness do not negate that dignity. No, this social justice concept is based on the principle of solidarity, which states that we are all inter-dependent. And those with greater opportunities or marketable talents are to help sustain others that God brings into their lives. The gifts from God given to you are not to pad your own lifestyle.

It's easy to shrug this off as being guilted into 'giving welfare' to those who simply aren't willing to work. You will be challenged on that. The money you've earned is to be given at *your* discretion. This includes amply providing for your own parish and their ministries; that's a basic Church precept...more to share on that later. So, begin this theme by recognizing simplicity in yourself and others. Then you will work through a reflection on simplifying your possessions, followed by considering your own desires for your future. An important journal will be your opportunity in considering an uncluttered life, or to imagine that style of light-living. To switch it up, you will look at simplifying your mind, and to help in that will be a reflection on the role of personal prayer. Finally, you will plan for a simple day—that is a whole day of 'lightness of heart'. This will reorient your perspectives and, in many ways, remove some heavy burdens. Consider it!

The Town Mouse and the Country Mouse is a famous Aesop Fable. The Country Mouse only had simple fare to offer his friend, so the Town Mouse invited him to where he lives as the food is both delicate and plenty. But upon arrival, and while feasting a creaking door sent both mice running for safety. The Country Mouse returned home saying how he would rather eat and live simply than have delicacies in the midst of fear and insecurity.

"The whole world being divided about whether the stream was going slower or faster, became conscious of something vague but vast...a dead thing can go with the stream, but only a living thing can go against it."

G. K. Chesterton in *The Everlasting Man*, 1925

JOURNAL 71

SIMPLICITY IN MYSELF AND OTHERS

"Blessed are you poor, for yours is the Kingdom of God" (Luke 6:20b)

Things to consider: Do you sometimes find yourself comparing your 'living style' to others? Not if others just have more than you, but also the judgmental notion of, "They have too much!" or "They're so rich...no one needs a house that big!" That raises the question, "What is too much?" "How much is rich?" It may be hard to believe, but there are likely others who think *you* have too much or are too rich. The correct question is, "What is necessary?" Are you aware of the stuff that fills your own life? Do you justify it by saying you sometimes need it, or it was given to you, or it was so cheap? One answer to "What is necessary?" is whether you're willing to give it away. It's very difficult and challenging with *things* to 'go backwards' or lower your standard of comfort and living. If you're accustomed to having your own bedroom with a private bath, then anything less seems not enough. If you're used to wonderful but expensive vacations, then just going for an overnight visit doesn't satisfy. Most generations want to do at least slightly better than the last...so everything gets bigger. In this journal challenge, what are the parameters for your threshold of simplicity? What do you deem *necessary*? Be critical and ask if those *bigger things* are genuinely worth all the hard work and long hours it takes to have them. How would living simpler make life easier to enjoy the 'free' things? Consider it!

MY CHALLENGE OF SIMPLICITY IN MYSELF & OTHERS

JOURNAL 72

SIMPLIFYING MY POSSESSIONS

"But woe to you that are rich, for you have received your consolation" (Luke 6:24)

Things to consider: Mentally picture what's in your bedroom, the family room, your garage and basement. How much of that 'stuff' do you think is necessary? Exclude what you *truly* need for school and/or work; but be critical. Estimate a ballpark figure of what it would cost to replace it all. Then add the cost of what else you own above the necessities; extra cars (does every driver *need* their own car?), clothing and shoes, yearly vacation(s), landscaping, electronics for entertainment, any recreational vehicles...you get the idea. Is it a lot? Jesus says in Matthew's Gospel, "Do not lay up for yourselves treasures on earth...where thieves break in and steal." What does that mean? Here's a personal story of mine. My late mother, an elderly Italian woman, lived in a part of town that had become infested with meth labs. Her house was broken into, thankfully while she was not home. Except for the $20 bill she had on her bureau for her next day's hair appointment, nothing was stolen. It's because there was nothing of material value to steal. She only had family photos, dollar store dishes and utensils, framed religious pictures and some statuary, modest furniture, a clock radio and a wall phone. There were no treasures *laid up* for thieves to break in and steal. What could be stolen from your house? What treasures have you laid up for thieves to steal? Where is your heart? Consider it!

MY CHALLENGE OF SIMPLIFYING MY POSSESSIONS

JOURNAL 73

SIMPLIFYING MY DESIRES FOR THE FUTURE

"For where your treasure is, there will your heart be also" (Matt. 6:21)

Things to consider: Nothing ever really goes as planned. Some Christians mistakenly think, "Whatever happens, it's *God's* will!" That pins a lot of bad choices people make on God. Something positive may come out of any and all bad choices you make, but don't blame the sufferings from your poor choices on God's will. Yet, as St. Paul states, "All things God works for the good of those who love Him." So, your future won't be perfect, yet your bad choices leave room for God to work. But concerning your future, the first question should be, "What is God calling you to do?" Most are scared to ask this. They think God might lead them to the choice *they* don't like. But if God can make good come from your *bad* choices, why doubt His guiding you in line with the charisms He gifted you with? Who better than He who created you to match your personality and charisms to an important life choice? This requires constant dialogue, not just with God but with those close to you...He works through them. The trick is to leave as many options open by simplifying your desires. Don't think in terms of marriage, but in terms of vocation. Don't think in terms of where you would like to live, but where you may be needed. Absolutely don't think in terms of potential salaries, but in terms of potential service to others. If asked by God, would you give up anything? Would you give up everything? Consider it!

MY CHALLENGE OF SIMPLIFYING MY FUTURE DESIRES

JOURNAL 74

SIMPLIFYING MY CLUTTERED LIFE

"For God is not a God of confusion, but of peace" (I Cor. 14:33)

Things to consider: The tragedy with a cluttered life is that any anxiety and stress from it is self-imposed. What consumes your time each week? The lives of young families are hectic, and the burdens of older households are often unsettled. In life, most try to squeeze things in for fun and leisure such as movies, going out to eat, meeting friends, etc. You're always trying to *fit in* as much as possible. If there's an opening, it becomes an opportunity to do 'one more thing'. Your days have been made busy but haven't led to a more fulfilling or meaningful life. The other tragedy is the sheer lack of solitude and silence that finds any regular place in the modern person's day or week. Not everyone likes to be alone with him or herself. What might that silence reveal? In the 21st century, it's impossible to address this issue without acknowledging the intrusion of cell phones and social media. It's said these things disconnect people from each other. It's more likely they disengage people from their own thoughts and become a 'destroyer of peace'. The accumulated clutter presently found in a person's day seems unparalleled. In simplifying a cluttered life, don't ask yourself what you have to 'give up', but in all the frenetic activity, what are you missing? What important things is your cluttered schedule taking away from your soul? Consider it!

MY CHALLENGE OF SIMPLIFYING MY CLUTTERED LIFE

_____

_____

_____

_____

_____

_____

_____

_____

_____

_____

_____

_____

_____

_____

_____

_____

_____

_____

_____

_____

_____

_____

_____

JOURNAL 75

SIMPLIFYING MY MIND

"The unfolding of thy words gives light" (Psalm 119:130)

Things to consider: Your mind needs order. Think of the call to be single-minded. You must have goals, but you must weigh pursuing those goals against the many other 'goods' in your life. St. Thomas Aquinas distinguished between *studiositas* and *curiositas*. Those Latin words carry the meaning of *diligence* and *escapism*. In the world of the Internet, almost every curiosity could be satisfied; who won the Super Bowl in 1972?, what country occupied modern day France in the early second century?, etc. This is known as trivia or a 'proud knowledge' and falls into the category of vice (*curiositas*). The knowledge could also be what Thomas called 'superstitious', i.e., it aligns with one's point of view, but is dubious. Think how in politics some swallow 'knowledge' that supports their candidate even if it's a half-truth. Sound harmless? Another type of disordered thinking is when someone attempts to make a claim to a truth outside of their competency. Not everyone is an expert in everything, so relying on an expert is fine. It's a way of getting information to assist one in thinking for one's self. Finally, there is nothing more disordered than seeking truths that make one materially wealthy or physically healthy but lose sight of beauty, truth and goodness. How do you unclutter and prioritize the pursuits of your mind? What 'trivia' captures your time? Your energy? Do you seek *escapism* or proud knowledge? Consider it!

MY CHALLENGE OF SIMPLIFYING MY MIND

JOURNAL 76

LOVING AND PERSONAL PRAYER

"This kind cannot be driven out by anything but prayer" (Mark 9:29)

Things to consider: Few people pray often enough. The reason typically revolves around available time—but just dismiss that fallacious reasoning. Admit that one's priorities are the culprit. Prayer is dialogue with God. In Fr. Thomas Dubay, S.M.'s book, *Prayer Primer: A Fire Within*, he points out that this longing of communicating for the infinite is unique to humans. Though plants and other animals may have a future perfection after this world passes away, there is not an inner longing for the transcendent.[15] For the human person, selfish pursuits and individual egoism satisfy only finite material longings, so you're really operating beneath your nature in that regard. With prayer, then, just like those dear ones in your life, nothing could be more natural than conversing with your uncreated eternal Beloved. Any rejection of God, therefore, is inevitable idolatry. Isn't being captivated by lesser things moving in that direction? So, entering into loving prayer is a response to *coming to the waters* with your thirst. That's an important illustration. Do you have a problem finding contentment in your life? It may be because you remain thirsty while there's a well full of water waiting for you. How is your prayer life? Do you even have a prayer life? How might prayer help unclutter your mind to simplify your life? Consider it!

My Challenge of Loving and Personal Prayer

JOURNAL 77

A WHOLE DAY OF LIGHTNESS OF HEART

"For from [your heart] flows the springs of life" (Proverbs 4:23b)

Things to consider: A quick return to this theme's previous challenges should remind you that the goal was to make room for love by simplifying aspects of your life. This included evaluating your possessions and desires for the future, and to focus on personal prayer as a way to re-orient your thinking and time. The risk now with considering a whole day of lightness of one's heart is to confuse the concept of 'lightness' with the concept of 'care-freeness'. It cannot simply be a day without deadlines or worries. Think of one's *heart* to mean *being*. But even if it shouldn't be a holiday, it might be best to plan for this day on a Sunday (Holy day) where there will be, or should be, fewer worldly distractions. Psalm 63 begins with these comforting words, "O God, thou art my God, I seek thee, my soul thirsts for thee; my flesh faints for thee, as in a dry and weary land where not water is. So, I have gazed upon thee in the sanctuary, beholding thy power and glory." Fix your 'gaze' on God, or from Him, something beautiful in nature, the woods, the ocean, etc., then re-consider how a cluttered life detracts from that peace. Bring yourself to a place where the burdens of the present and future recede? Contemplative prayer has the ability to transport you and offer some respite even in a busy world? Try it. What will you fix your gaze on to quench your thirsting soul? Plan your day of lightness of being. Consider it!

MY WHOLE DAY OF LIGHTNESS OF HEART

THEME TWELVE: LETTING GO OF ANGER FOR PEACE

Following Dr. Ronda's lead from the introduction to the reflections of this theme in the original *Way of Love*, let's be reminded that the third theme was about opening yourself to loving forgiveness by overcoming resentment. That week was primarily about *large* causes of anger. This week is more about everyday irritations that seem to make peace nothing but an impossible ideal. So, this theme will address those other *lesser* aspects that contribute to anger. If it's true, as they say, that the devil is in the details, then ferreting out those details that have buried themselves under hardened habits is likely even more important than identifying the previous larger issues.

Perhaps an example would be to think about times when you've claimed a fact during a conversation (talking about when something happened in history, or how long it took to drive somewhere). Say the person you're speaking with is obviously incorrect but refuses to concede they're wrong even if you point the date out in a textbook, or show them some proof of the mileage. Aren't you tempted to bring in another person to verify you're correct? And if you find the 'proof' later, can you hardly wait to see them again and show them the *facts*? What devil is in those details? You're correct and know it. The 'detail' missed is that reconciliation is better than vindication. That vindication may be a 'little victory,' but your victory will be at the expense of peace and friendship.

The above issue is minor. But remember this theme is about the lesser irritations. Keep that in mind as you move through these reflections. Psychologists say that anger is linked to fear. It's that primal flight-or-fight mechanism that stirs up emotions to defend, bark back or stand your ground. That's not the sum of it, but the instinct to maintain control is ever present and a contributing factor. If the information in your conversations seems to be regularly questioned, or often dismissed without being 'fact' checked, the discomfort will only build up like a pressure cooker in you. At some point, it's too much and you start bringing highlighted encyclopedia pages and a GPS device around.

So, what's the typical *relief valve* to keep things from getting ready to blow? In order for you to diffuse your pent-up anger, you might resort to name-calling under your breath—calling them a jerk or referring to them as a smart aleck every time they walk past. You might even become a wiseacre yourself and perhaps when they walk up to you say, "Hey, should we argue over how much time it took for you to get here?" And it won't be long before the snide comments migrate to your talking about them behind their back. These are your 'little victories'. And well...at this point the other person's in your head. You'll wonder how something petty became an issue. You'll long for the peace and friendship there was between you...if you would've only smiled when they said, "Columbus sailed the ocean blue in 1592," instead of having to prove them wrong. You probably have your own examples.

In this theme of letting go of anger for peace, you will begin by observing those two specific things in your life. You will be asked to identify the peaceful fruits of resignation as opposed to rage and do your best to understand the motives of others. You'll reflect on how excusing rather than accusing offers the fruits of peace and how using loving and gentle speech does not allow anger to get a foot hold in your heart and soul. Not to be forgotten, you will consider the power of prayer in working toward peaceful solutions of the conflicts in your life. Then finally per the design of so many of these themes, you will set out to plan an entire day of peace. Is that possible? Could be. Consider it!

Aesop's Fable offers a lesson in anger. In The Bear and the Bees, the Bear was after the honey. The few Bees that stung him while he plundered their hives were only an annoyance. But as the whole swarm attacked the Bear, his swatting in anger proved to be of little relief to the stings he suffered by the many Bees who annoyed his eyes and pierced his thick hide.

"God simply refused to answer, and somehow the question is answered. Job flings at God one riddle, God flings back at Job a hundred riddles, and Job is at peace."

G. K. Chesterton in *The Speaker,* 1905

JOURNAL 78

OBSERVING PEACEFULNESS AND ANGER

"To set the mind on the Spirit is life and peace" (Romans 8:6b)

Things to consider: There was a show on TV years ago called Candid Camera. They were pranking guests at a hotel during a PBS convention. Once the bellman set the luggage down in the room of the unsuspecting *victim*, he would wait to see if they noticed there was no TV in the room—after all, this was a PBS convention and he thought that would get them angry. You could imagine the reactions, "How can a hotel not have a workable TV, so either fix it or bring another." Now, it just happened that one of the *victims* coincidently turned out to be the TV children's show personality, Mr. Fred Rogers. He didn't notice the missing TV, but when told about it, he ironically responded, "That's perfectly fine. I don't watch TV." They couldn't make him angry. They commented afterwards that he could lower one's blood pressure simply by entering a room. What would it be like to have such a personality? Are you or others easily upset? How do you observe peacefulness and anger in yourself or those around you? What makes you angry? What do others do to make you feel peaceful? What fruits does peace bear? Or does anger create? Consider it!

MY CHALLENGE OF OBSERVING PEACE AND ANGER

JOURNAL 79

RESIGNATION VS. RAGE

"As far as it depends on you, live peaceably with all" (Romans 12:17)

Things to consider: Doesn't *resignation* connote that something bad happened, and you resigned out of weakness to give up something you really liked? But there's another understanding of the word. To *resign* yourself means accepting something undesirable or even inevitable. There's nothing weak in the strength necessary to do that. It's actually a mark of maturity. So, when you're in a situation (recall peace is the goal) where the choice is to resign yourself to the fact the other person won't or will not change his or her behavior or they will not listen to reason, remember that *you're* the stronger person. Flip the position. What if instead of resigning yourself to the fact there's no way to resolve the situation, you went into a fit of rage? Rage, by definition is uncontrollable. Where's the strength in that? In the end, this is a matter of *your* will. Even when you're in the right (the car in front of you is going 10 mph under the speed limit, or your friend is inconsiderate and rude), you cannot *will* the car to go faster, or *will* the friend to become considerate. Your choice is to resign (accept) the case, or be consumed with rage. Focus on that last sentence. Write in your reflection when you've allowed someone else's weakness to 'consume' you. Think, too, of the time when you chose resignation. Which brought peace? Which took more strength? How does this all relate to love? Consider it!

MY CHALLENGE OF CONSIDERING RESIGNATION

Journal 80

Understanding Other's Motives

"Let not your hearts be troubled, neither let them be afraid" (John 14:27b)

Things to consider: There are two general reasons to question another's motives. The first is you may have a rational reason to suspect *they* are misleading you by persuasion or even outright deceit, i.e., they've done it before, body cues, etc. That requires acumen on your part. The second reason aligns more to *your* dispositions, i.e., you have some personal defect, a level of ignorance on a topic or just free-floating reluctance from prior bad experiences. Two examples on guessing motives: On being misled—you and your friend are watching a TV infomercial that claims while being able to eat what you want, a wonder diet pill can shed pounds without exercise. Your friend says, "It worked for me." Because he had a Cheshire grin and is always the expert, you conclude he's exaggerating, and his motive is to convince you the spurious claim is true. The other on your personal defect—but what if you were a late-night infomercial junkie? It's your weakness—the healing therapy magnets and 120 pc. knife set proves it. Plus, you have a personal defect of optimism mixed with gullibility. Now when your friend says, "It worked for me," you think his sarcasm is pointing out how easily you're deceived, and you become defensive. Both had the same response, but differed only in how you assessed the situation and responded. So, do you take comments personally? In what ways do you defend your weaknesses? Do you 'read into' other's remarks? Consider it!

My Challenge of Understanding Motives

JOURNAL 81

EXCUSING INSTEAD OF ACCUSING

"Let us pursue what makes for peace and mutual upbuilding" (Romans 14:19)

Things to consider: When you hear a smoke detector beeping because the battery needs to be changed, do you yell at it? Or when it goes off just because some spilled-over food at the bottom of the oven is smoking? There's a joke that someone should invent a smoke alarm that shuts off by yelling, "I'm just cooking!" But, in reality, aren't you just *accusing* the smoke detector of simply doing its job? More seriously, does it irritate you when there's construction on the road and the flag person happens to stop allowing cars through just as you approach? Maybe you've blamed a coach for working you hard—he or she was conditioning you; or a teacher was being demanding—he or she wanted to elevate you out of ignorance; or a doctor telling you to lay off the snacks—your health was his or her concern. It's easy to simply accuse those people of making you do things you don't like. Have you ever considered these relationships as *encounters*? According to the Austrian-born Jewish existentialist Martin Buber, all *encounters* are essential for growth and development. They form the sum of life. [16] You will be more likely to *accuse* someone viewed as an object (an *It* that is telling you what to do), and *excuse* someone viewed as another you (a *Thou* that wants what is best for you). What are your experiences, your *encounters* of accusing others? What helps you 'excuse' them? Consider it!

226

My Challenge of Excusing Others

JOURNAL 82

LOVING, GENTLE SPEECH

"Blessed are the peacemakers, they shall be called sons of God" (Mt. 5:9)

Things to consider: In the theme on giving advice, it was stated that the etymology for *gentle* is from the Latin and can have the connotation of being of the same family, or of a noble birth. That adds a nice dimension here to the common definition of gentle, which is to not be harsh in manner or speech. It seems to suggest that it's not just about speaking softly or tenderly, but placing all people present on the same level...of one *family*. So, loving, gentle speech is about tender speech. But it cannot include you speaking 'down' to another; all deserve respect. It should be understood that in this reflection, what is being addressed is not simply speaking about what is good, but speaking in a good way to those recognized as your equal. Seeing another as an equal always sets the tone for a conversation. Any well-formed rational argument has the potential to change another's mind, but an improper tone may be a turn off. With loving and gentle speech, there is a chance it may make its way not just into the other's mind, but also into the other's heart. Gentle speech disarms the other person. It allows what you say to overcome a defensive attitude. Reflect on a time when your speech was not received well due to your tone. Was there another time when you spoke gently and lovingly, and that made all the difference? How do you respond to another's tone? Consider it!

My Challenge of Loving and Gentle Speech

JOURNAL 83

PEACEFUL SOLUTIONS TO CONFLICTS

"The LORD lift up his countenance upon you, and give you peace" (Num. 6:26)

Things to consider: It may not be your first thought to 'pray' for a peaceful solution to a conflict. Most people are 'doers' and think that working toward a resolution or the way out of a conflict is only by action. Stopping to pray seems a waste of time. But on the natural level, even the self-reflection that happens during prayer and meditation is a good thing. Perhaps by letting a little time lapse, things may 'cool' down. But add the dynamic of prayer, and one introduces the Father's wisdom, the example of the Son and the Spirit's grace. That changes you. Peace is not the absence of conflict. It is something that must be pursued and maintained. Peace is very much connected to your personality. Introspection and peace are interrelated. That's where praying for peace comes in...it involves first refreshing one's own mind and heart. Peace in the world truly does begin with each individual. Then peace in the person helps build peace in the family, in the community, in the country and so on. The Hebrews' understanding of peace (*shalom*) has the sense of 'restoring'. Perhaps this is referring to an equilibrium that is often missing in the modern person's hectic life. So, restore peace first in yourself, then address the conflict. Was there a time you jumped into resolving a personal conflict without reflection? Did it help? Did it make things worse? How could prayer and reflection have helped? Consider it!

MY CHALLENGE OF PEACEFUL SOLUTIONS

JOURNAL 84

ONE WHOLE DAY OF PEACE

"And let the peace of Christ rule in your hearts" (Col. 3:15)

Things to consider: Imagine what a whole day of peace would be like? Would it be a sublime, magical day with no pressing commitments, totally void of anxiety? If a day of peace is a day without conflicts, that would make peace impossible. You cannot control life's emergencies or circumstances. You can manage the anxieties by realizing that peace is primarily *your* responsibility. Peace starts with you, and this planning day could be one of the hundreds of *new beginnings* you will have throughout your life. You began by observing peace and anger. Then you were asked to identify the peaceful fruits of resignation rather than rage. Though not easy, you tried your best to understand the motives of others. With the help of Martin Buber, you learned how excusing rather than accusing offers the fruits of peace. There was also a reflection about how using loving and gentle speech could defuse a situation, while responding with a 'tone' or using harsh language would exacerbate it. The last reflection was on how praying for peaceful solutions to conflicts may seem like a waste of time but should really be your first consideration. So, how will you map out your day of peace? In what ways can you 'grow' into being an instrument of peace for a whole day? Can you change your *world*? Can you change *you* in your world? Consider it!

MY WHOLE DAY OF PEACE

_____
_____
_____
_____
_____
_____
_____
_____
_____
_____
_____
_____
_____
_____
_____
_____
_____
_____
_____
_____
_____
_____
_____
_____

THEME THIRTEEN: COOPERATIVE VS. BOSSY

Not all relationships are democratic. In some relations, one group inherently holds the authority, such as those of parents over children, instructors over students, employers over employees, officers of the law over citizens, etc. In those instances, cooperation is typically understood not just in terms of compliancy, but also out of respect for the authority inherent in the *higher* position. Provided the request is legitimate and reasonable, to dismiss the authority in each is to disrespect and undermine the institutions of family, teaching, employment or the law. A child might not like to be *told* to help with the dishes; a student doesn't want to be *instructed* to sit down; not all employees want to hear they've been *assigned* to a project; and a citizen pulled over for speeding may resent being *ordered* to provide his or her license and registration. But cooperation in these unequal relationships does not wane because someone is bossy.

If you research the etymology of the word *cooperate,* you'll learn it has the meaning of uniting in one body for a single purpose. It is derived from the Latin *corporare,* which is the transitive verb meaning to *form* into a body. So, to *cooperate* is to bring together, and by contrast being *bossy* is to separate or divide. In the previous scenarios, bossiness doesn't just divide the two personally involved, but it ultimately creates divisions in the stability of the institutions that inherently provided the authority.

But it's different peer-to-peer. The relationship between two students, workers, drivers on the road, or a shopper and clerk at the checkout line, is not predicated on any hierarchy of authority. Even the clerk does not *work* for you. But the common goals of education, employment, safe travel and orderly commerce can be undermined by bossy behavior. And the similarity between the two types of relationships reveals the *culprit* of bossiness. That is, someone is asserting his or her *ego* over the other. Having an *ego* isn't bad; in fact, it's necessary. Your *ego* is simply *you*. It's all the collective aspects of your in-born nature and those experiences throughout life. That is generally understood to be the case by the Jungian school of analytical psychology.

So anytime you say "I," you are speaking of your *ego*, or that you are an individual. The urge to be bossy rather than cooperative is when this *ego* turns selfish and destroys the harmony of your relationships; the term *ego*-tistical is fitting. But add traits such as being controlling and manipulative, and you have the recipe for a narcissist. In each case of the child, student, employee or citizen, his or her self-interest took precedence over the good of the overall institution or relationship. This has a collective and somewhat corroding effect. Over time, these relations don't just become unstable; they also present deteriorating outcomes for the bossy individual. The other becomes an 'It.' Additionally, moral permissiveness because your own weaknesses, whenever you see them appear in others, become easier to tolerate.

That might have been a lot to digest. Don't worry, as this theme will help pull out those meanings. You will be asked to ferret out various distinctions in your own life, first by observing cooperative and bossy behavior in yourself and others. You will specifically identify inappropriate stances of authority and consider how offering help in daily circumstances fosters cooperation. You will be asked to not be upset when your own authority is ignored and to consider having a quiet spirit and recognize the joy of being in the background. As you might suspect, this reflection will wrap up with your planning a whole day of being cooperative with love for others as your goal. Consider it!

When a storm arrives, an Oak tree is strong and sturdy, whereas the Reeds though lighter and weak can bend more easily in the wind. Aesop's The Oak and The Reeds teaches that allowing oneself to cooperate with the torrents in life is far better in the end, and that unlike the rigid Oak tree, they remain standing after the storm subsides.

"Complete self-confidence in not merely a sin; complete self-confidence is a weakness."

G. K. Chesterton in *Orthodoxy*, 1908

Journal 85

Observing Cooperation vs. Bossiness

"When each part is working properly [the body] upbuilds itself" (Eph. 4:16b)

Things to consider: Begin this reflection by identifying various relationships in your life. Pick one where you are subordinate in authority, and another where you have the duty to legitimately require something of another person. What do or did you observe in those relationships concerning bossiness and cooperation? How did it differ depending on the dynamic of your relationship...be specific? Whether it was you or the other person, was authority wielded around in some display of superiority? Or was the one in the *superior* role humbled by their responsibility, recognizing that both were working towards a 'common goal'? Now think of an instance where no legitimate authority was present. Was the other person(s) becoming your target? Were they simply an outlet for pressured feelings that were building up in your life? Finally, when you were in any relationship or situation where everyone was on the same level, were you consciously aware that the purpose was to work towards the common goal? There will be more 'analysis' on these points throughout this theme. In the meantime, see if you can't identify a concrete instance or situation where you observed cooperative vs. bossy behavior in your life, both when legitimate authority was present and also in your peer-to-peer relations. Consider it!

My Challenge of Observing Cooperation

_____

_____

_____

_____

_____

_____

_____

_____

_____

_____

_____

_____

_____

_____

_____

_____

_____

_____

_____

_____

_____

_____

_____

_____

JOURNAL 86

INAPPROPRIATE STANCES OF SUPERIORITY

"And [know] there is no partiality with God" (Eph. 6:9b)

Things to consider: In St. Paul's Letter to the Romans, there's that enigmatic line which reads, "Let every person be subject to the governing authorities. For there is no authority except from God." On the surface, you might immediately wonder if this applies to those ruthless dictators. Must all citizens under some totalitarian rule concede that God has given power to a despot? The Jesuit Biblical scholar, Brendan Byrne, S.J., in his commentary on that passage in the *Sacra Pagina* series points out that it ultimately means no government (or any person) is a 'law unto themselves'; rather, all authority is ultimately answerable to God.[17] The power you might have, whether it is where you work, teach, go to school, or remain at your home may be minimal, but some personalities wield any little power they have over others. It's a test of character, and the bossy person typically yields to the thirst for control. For some, this control is addictive. But there's a positive motive for legitimate stances of superiority, too, and that is ultimately *love*. Being lovingly responsible for others carries an obligation of control. This loving control is never manipulative, but always guiding. Rather than increasing one's power and image as in the case of the despot, appropriate stances of superiority are to be respected. Think of a time when someone either 'controlled' you with their authority or 'loved' you with the responsibility they have for you. Consider it!

MY CHALLENGE OF STANCES OF AUTHORITY

Journal 87

Offering Help in Daily Circumstances

"You have need of endurance [to] do the will of God" (Heb. 10:36)

Things to consider: Your first consideration here might be how you help your family, friends, coworkers, fellow students, etc. That's important. Too often, though, you might find yourself being nicer and putting your 'best face' on for strangers. It's not a bad thing to want others to think well of you. But those who are closest in your life, do they get your best? They do need your help and assistance in daily tasks, but they especially require the emotional support that comes from knowing they can count on you. To require them to question that support, or to require them to constantly prod you to help them whittles down trust. It will, moreover, cause others to question your motives when you do help in those daily circumstances. So, when it comes to cleaning the house, taking care of the yard work, or putting away the leftovers after a meal, do you have to be constantly asked to help? And if you live in a house with others, why would you consider those things as *helping*? Isn't it your house, too? Now what about helping those 'strangers' in your life? Do you try to sneak ahead in merging traffic? When you're shopping, do you return products to where they belong, or tuck them onto the nearest shelf? Take a mental walk through the last week of your life. How did you help others in their daily circumstances? In what ways can you improve? Consider it!

MY CHALLENGE OF OFFER HELP DAILY

JOURNAL 88

ACCEPTANCE OF IGNORED AUTHORITY

"Judge not...the measure you give will be the measure you get" (Mt. 7:1a, 2b)

Things to consider: Everyone is under someone else's authority; otherwise, your life and world would be anarchy. Think of how a world without any leadership would be a waste of the great talents so many people possess, and how the authority would only go to those who have power. This is true whether it's concerning a country, a work environment, a classroom or a family. Recall that genuine authority comes from God and is accountable to Him. And it should be exercised with the same amount of love He has for all of His creation. You are under someone's authority and may often forget that by the time you've been asked to do something at work, or learn something in class, much thought and contemplation has already occurred, i.e., the lesson preparation and planning meeting is over, and now you're being asked to submit to authority. The cardinal virtue of Prudence has three primary acts (potential parts), counsel, judgment and command. Counsel includes all the research, contemplation and information gathering. If you're not *in charge*, that's the part you don't see. If you are *in charge*, that's the part the employee or student doesn't see. Everyone may like to have their input considered, but even if the employee or student prefers collaborating with their teacher or employer rather than following what seems an arbitrary command, legitimate authority cannot be ignored. How are you with authority? Consider it!

_____
_____
_____
_____
_____
_____
_____
_____
_____
_____
_____
_____
_____
_____
_____
_____
_____
_____
_____
_____
_____
_____

Journal 89

Having a Quiet Spirit

"Be the hidden person of the heart with...a gentle and quiet spirit" (1 Pt. 3:4)

Things to consider: The idea of 'quiet' is being lost in the present generation. The reasons are probably legion, but the anxieties of life and constant lure of distraction are certainly the culprits. Sometimes, life is hard to deal with, and being busy and distracted provides cushion to a harsh reality. But motives and goals can also be great distractions as you might think you *need* to join clubs, or *need* to rise higher in your career path, or *need* to remodel the house, or *need* to landscape the yard, or *need* to detail your car, etc. An old saying is that there are more important things in life than rearranging one's sock drawer. Clubs, careers, remodeling and so on, are good things; even the sock drawer needs to be rearranged at some point. But when these things fill your day and distract you from being alone with yourself, there's no room to nurture a quiet spirit. Having a quiet spirit is regularly confronting the great ideas of life, the quality of your friendships, your vocation, etc. The fruit of these things is not just peace but understanding. It contributes to other important areas in your life. Such reflection helps so that when you are conversing with someone, it will be to understand and not to impress them. Your speaking will add to a conversation, not tear down or wound. You will find beauty, truth and goodness in places hidden from those who frenetically chase empty solace in life's rat race. How has life's noise been allowed to steal your quiet spirit? Consider it!

MY CHALLENGE OF HAVING A QUIET SPIRIT

_____

_____

_____

_____

_____

_____

_____

_____

_____

_____

_____

_____

_____

_____

_____

_____

_____

_____

_____

_____

_____

_____

_____

JOURNAL 90

ENJOYING BEING IN THE BACKGROUND

"The Spirit bears witness with our spirit...we are children of God" (Rom. 8:16)

Things to consider: Sometimes, people who seek the spotlight are doing it for other's elation. They're the *jokesters* who want to bring laughter into the room and joy to your heart. Other times, unfortunately, there are those who love being on center stage, not content unless all eyes and ears are on them. Different motives for sure, but isn't it nice just being in the audience? The performer always has a different experience; the *encounter* doesn't unfold in front of them. With a narcissist, they think all people in the 'background' are *extras,* casted to support them in their leading role. Staying in the background helps you enjoy the jokester and shields you as much as possible from the egomaniac. But being in the background is not synonymous with indifference or shyness. It's about listening, reflecting and engaging only to make a point of truth or clarify an error. Saying nothing is sometimes the best response. That is the point in the Aesop Fable, "The Owls, the Bats, and the Sun." The birds are mocking the Sun. The Sun, though able to destroy the birds, responds that the only revenge he will take is to shine on them. [18] Finally, it would be remiss to not mention technology's assault on silence. Some always have a TV on, checking their phones, have earbuds in, etc. They're not 'in the background;' they're sluggish and not present. How are you in the background, hearing with your ears? With your eyes? With your mind and spirit? Consider it!

MY CHALLENGE OF BEING IN THE BACKGROUND

_____

_____

_____

_____

_____

_____

_____

_____

_____

_____

_____

_____

_____

_____

_____

_____

_____

_____

_____

_____

_____

_____

JOURNAL 91

BEING COOPERATIVE ALL DAY LONG

"[Be] eager to maintain the unity of the Spirit in the bond of peace" (Eph. 4:3)

Things to consider: This is not the last theme, but this will be the last day-long exercise. Here is a short recap on this theme. Recall that the etymology of the word *cooperate* has the meaning of uniting for a single purpose. You were asked to observe both cooperative and bossy behavior and, closely related, to identify inappropriate stances of authority in various occurrences. Then you were to consider offering help in daily circumstances, considering the relation between support and trust. The thorny issue of authority, its origin in God and your ultimate accountability to Him summed up the next reflection. The last two journals were meant to orient you to be cooperative in terms of having a quiet spirit. And finally, like the powerful Sun of Aesop's Fable, to recognize not only the joy of being in the background, but knowing it is sometimes best to just *shine on them* in silence. For a strong ending to this theme, you are to map out a day this week to put all this into practice. Make it a day you will only speak if you can truly add to a conversation. How will you listen with your heart that day? Will you respect other's legitimate authority? How about drawing others towards a common good goal, rather than just asserting your own authority? Make it a day where your single goal is unity, for love's sake. Consider it!

My Whole Day of Being Cooperative

_____

_____

_____

_____

_____

_____

_____

_____

_____

_____

_____

_____

_____

_____

_____

_____

_____

_____

_____

_____

_____

THEME FOURTEEN: ON YOUR WORST DEFECT

This theme will be unlike any of the previous themes in the *Ways of Love* you have reflected on thus far. It's likely this will be the most emotionally draining and require the greatest level of self-reflection and critique. It is also the last, so you will need to stick with it in order to finish well. The theme introduction will also be slightly longer to accommodate the preparation necessary for your journal exercises. If it seems too 'deep' or heavy for you, then skim over it. As you read, don't think you need to comprehend all the points in order to properly work through the last reflections well. Just focus on the questions. Keep the parts that sink in and appear insightful and sift out the points that do not provide a connection. Perhaps in subsequent years, you will gain more from these densely packed journal considerations.

After this theme introduction, every reflection that follows will surround one personal defect you'll identify in yourself. You will be asked to unmask your worst defect, and that *one* trait will be dealt with and carried through the entire theme. Do not start thinking about that now, as it will be the focus of the second reflection—though you will gain much insight in identifying that defect from the following paragraphs. And don't suppose this will be a dark theme. The first and last reflections are quite positive, and, hopefully, they will act as *bookends* that will both buffer and keep your thoughtful analysis in perspective, oriented to love.

The idea for this topic is that over the course of the previous thirteen themes, it's likely you began to narrow down at least in a general way, some recurring issues that hinder you from lovingly approaching others in your life. No one is perfect, including you, so that defect should not come as a surprise. You're not Christ! It doesn't mean there is something *wrong* with you, only that you're a human being living in the world with other human beings. The structure or technique that is being employed here is for you to work through the seven Capital Vices (a.k.a. Deadly Sins)[19] and what they briefly encompass. Also, in those categories of vice, you will find mentioned specific countering virtues that help overcome the behavior or defective habit. So, a *way out* will be addressed in each section of vice before you move onto the reflections proper. Hopefully, that will send a signal that it's not all bad. Once you've identified a defect, you've begun the journey of overcoming it. That's good news. This is about character assessment; it isn't about determining if you have some psychiatric diagnoses; histrionic personality disorder, obsessive-compulsive personality disorder, etc. Remember, *this is not therapy*. The concern here is your character, considering your worst defect, and then overcoming it with courage and grace. Remember, you're not changing the world; you are only changing *you* in the world.

There will be some general questions posed at the end of each section to help you consider how and if that vice (defect) appears prominently in your life. If you find something that presents itself as an insight into your defects, jot it down. It is hoped that through the course of your reading something will be singled out specifically, or at least you could narrow down a few defects present in your life, and from those focus on just one for this theme. Conquer yourself in steps! The remedy is not unlike the acquired defect in that they both take time to develop. All habits, good or bad practices, or fostering vice or virtue in your character are formed incrementally. Seek your change from Him in which "there is no variation or shadow due to change."[20] Consider it!

Lust is typically listed first, though not intended to rank as the most serious. This vice is to accompany those things in life of which you derive pleasure, typically in terms of the venereal act (sexual deviancy). First, sex is a good; it is needed to propagate the human species and certainly an expression of love within marriage. Aquinas points out that "where there is the greatest necessity [you must] observe the order of reason." [21] He means that only reason and understanding can reveal the proper use of things sexual. In other words, both the human and other animals share an instinct to continue the species. But what separates you from the animal is your rational nature, i.e., you need not be a slave to your instincts. You can connect sex to love.

Chastity is the virtue needed need to counter Lust. Chastity is not abstinence. Chastity is properly ordered love according to one's vocation in life. Therefore, the single, married or even the consecrated religious person may all be chaste. What Chastity does is place as paramount the love of God, rather than relinquishing its priority to an earthly or corporeal love. The needs of the latter are to always serve the former.

Questions: In what ways do you look for the easy way out? Are people objects to you? In what ways do you let your animal instincts control you? Do you image God as a rational being? Do you comprehend how your own rationality is a participation in God's nature? Does your love of others image God, or do you simply look to satisfy your pleasure? Is it at someone else's expense? Consider it!

Gluttony is the second capital vice. Like lust, this vice perverts something good and necessary. Again, reason is set aside and not permitted to rationally regulate the self-preservation which man shares with all animals. In many ways, a glutton is acting like a brute. This, along with Lust is a sin of the flesh. Aquinas lists six daughters of Gluttony: dullness of one's senses (lack understanding), unseemly and excessive joy (immoderate appetite), loquaciousness (excessive or smooth talking), scurrility (rude or abusive language) and uncleanness. Cassian speaks of Gluttony as the foundational vice and points out that you "should chastise [your] body and bring it into subjection."[22]

Temperance is the antidote to this vice. It is a cardinal virtue. The word cardinal comes from the Latin word *cardo*, meaning *hinge*. Temperance is a properly ordered love of self. This virtue regulates those necessary things in life. Because this vice is a perversion of something truly good and necessary, it is typically thought to be a less culpable defect. To be excessively moderate too is a fault, as you are not to reject pleasure to the point of omitting what is necessary for the preservation of your own life and good.

Questions: So how are you with the obvious understanding of this vice? Are you controlled by food? Is pleasure the motivation to eat? How is the use of your language? Is it foul and abusive? How about in the other direction, do you over-exercise or sometimes starve yourself? How do *you* love yourself? Are you a partier, over-doing the fun? Are you a smooth talker? Do you subject your body to reason, or does it subject you? Consider it!

Greed is the third vice. It should be understood as the inordinate love for riches. Thomas Aquinas refers to it as covetousness and points out those things that are "good consist in a due measure, [and any evil use] ensues through excess or deficiency of that measure."[23] In short, the error is either too much or too little. This should not be difficult to recognize how it appears in your life. Cassian points out that this Greed approaches, "the soul from without [and is] more easily guarded against and resisted [but once in] the heart only with greater difficulty is it expelled."[24]

Generosity is the virtue opposed to the vice of Greed. This virtue is sometimes referred to as *liberality*. Those traits fall under the cardinal virtue of Justice, which itself means to give another their due. So, aspects of liberality are motivated by mercy and pity, seen as due to another person. Be watchful that rather than mercy or pity, you are led by the false motivations of being generous when you do so for the sake of boasting or to gain the esteem of others.

Questions: Do you consume more than necessary? Think of what you throw away each day. What could be saved? Do you give of yourself and your time freely? Do you donate to worthy and efficient charities? Do you give from your 'want' or just the excess that's left over? What have you let *into* your heart? Is it love, kindness and generosity? Or are you worried about 'having things'? Do you think your house and car speak highly of you? Do you compare your status to others? Do you give, but usually only when there is recognition? Do all your charity events or fundraisers include photos and team T-shirts? Consider it!

Sloth is the vice that includes laziness. It would incorporate avoiding physical responsibilities, necessary labor whether at work or at home, along with idleness and restlessness. But Sloth specifically refers to a spiritual laziness. Cassian warns that men can 'lose themselves in their affairs and business, thus little by little ensnared by dangerous occupation." [25] Aquinas quotes from St. John Damascene, who wrote in a gloss of Psalm 106:18 that Sloth is a "sluggishness of the mind which neglects to begin good."[26] Of the many disturbances this vice causes, among them Aquinas notes a two-fold effect from sorrow that basically means you might *avoid* good things if they are perceived to diminish your spirit, but yet *pass over* good things to seek those that simply bring more pleasure.

Diligence wards off sloth. It is also simply said that in Persistence or Perseverance, sloth wanes. Perseverance, along with Magnanimity (greatness with a notion of difficulty) and Patience (which steels you against various kinds of afflictions) are potential parts of the cardinal virtue called Fortitude. That virtue of Fortitude is defined as endurance in pursuit of a difficult good. So, the good you're working toward shouldn't be easy to attain, hence the need for persistence. To resist Sloth, you must *stick with it.*

Questions: Do you persevere in your tasks? Do you avoid things you should do? Does pleasure get you to do things you probably wouldn't do? How's your spirituality with Christ? Are you busy with work, and lazy with your faith? Do you do the minimal necessary to 'get' into heaven? Do you 'cave in' easily from a diminished spirit? Consider it!

Anger is the fifth capital vice. It is usually referred to as *Wrath*. Among the evils that this passion produces, Cassian lists as the inability to "acquire right judgment and discretion, be partakers of wisdom, and have clear judgment of heart or ripeness of counsel."[27] This is a vice that destroys not just peace, but the ability to be free of all types of disturbances. Once again, St. Thomas Aquinas speaks of 'six daughters' attributed to the vice of Anger. The first is indignation (anger with the unworthy), swelling of the mind (thoughts of vengeance), clamor (confused speech), blasphemy or contumely (depending if it is against God or neighbor) and quarrels (inflicted injuries).[28]

Meekness is what destroys anger within man's heart. Like clemency that counters Envy, Meekness, too, is a secondary virtue under Temperance. Meekness moderates anger as it appears in your soul. Christ says in the eleventh chapter of Matthew's Gospel, "Learn from me, for I am gentle (meek) and lowly of heart, and you will find rest for your souls." It's really Christ's burden—let Him share it. Anger is often simply a reaction to frustration. It would be a shame if you brought those disturbances on yourself.

Questions: So, are you prone to anger? Is resistance and confrontation frequent in your life? Do you curse a lot just to vent? Do you lack a gentle soul in discussions with others? Do you have an angry heart? Do you think things through before reacting? Do you tend to rant and rave or cause disturbances? Are you prone to return evil for evil? Do you plot on how to 'get back' at someone? Consider it!

Envy is the sixth capital vice. Philosophically it is not identical with jealousy. The distinction there is that with jealousy you do not want someone to take what is yours. You *jealously* protect 'it, him or her'; *they're mine,* you might think. Envy doesn't simply desire what belongs to someone else but goes further wishing them discomfort or loss. For example, if you can't have 'it, him or her,' then you hope neither can the other person. Aquinas explains this point by stating how this vice wishes to 'diminish the good name' of the other so "that a man is envious of those only whom he wishes to rival or surpass in reputation."[29] The return of anger to those whom you envy will only increase strife.

Kindness diminishes the lure of envy. Kindness is a practice and is also referred to by the term *clementia.* You can see the etymology of *clemency* in that Latin word. Kindness moderates the anger of anyone ready to punish or sentence another. This, along with meekness and modesty, is known as potential or secondary parts of the cardinal virtue of Temperance. Modesty regulates those things somewhat easier to control, and meekness moderates anger in one's soul. This is about properly loving yourself.

Questions: So, do you take pleasure in other's suffering when you don't get your way? Do you compare yourself materially with others and want to 'beat' them at having more? If someone has what you want, do you wish suffering or loss on them, out of spite? Are you always worried that someone else will take what's yours? Do you lack kindness? Would you suffer for not having something? Do you know how to properly love yourself? Consider it!

Pride is the last and chief of all the vices. According to Aquinas, from it comes the inordinate "desire for one's own excellence."[30] Pride makes all other vices and sin possible. There are three general ways in which vice enters one's heart and habit. First is through ignorance, in that you did not know the truth. That does not acquit you; there are some truths that *cannot not be known* (natural law). The second is from weakness. Whether it originates from fear or despair, weakness is a vice. Thirdly, and most wickedly, the vice of Pride appears as contempt or disdain not just for others but also for truth and wisdom as it is found in God. Consider as an example the line from John Milton's *Paradise Lost*, "Better to reign in Hell, than serve in Heaven."[31]

Humility counters this vice. Humility is really an honest self-assessment, and not the depreciating sense of character as is often popularly thought. Humility is not 'putting yourself down' but includes patience and perspective. Cassian points out that if you considered yourself "inferior to every one else [you] would bear everything offered, even if hurtful, and saddening, and damaging—with the utmost

260

patience."[32] So it begs a type of submissiveness. It's knowing your origin in and reliance on God. *Humility* is the mother of all virtues, fittingly paired against *Pride*, the root of all vice.

Questions: Are you contemptuous if others don't recognize your talents? Do you think you know best? Do you know your talents originate in God? Are you better than everyone, but never say it out load? Would you rather have life your way, and hope God understands? Consider it.

There are many philosophical, psychological and spiritual influences underneath the considerations being offered in the *Ways of Love.* You may have only been aware of those that were quoted or directly cited thus far. But here's one not previously mentioned. It's from Dante Alighieri's "Inferno," the first book of *The Divine Comedy.* The *Commedia* has run as a thread throughout this entire book. First a brief lead-up that sets the stage for the point. The occupants of the inferno, a.k.a. those that have died, willingly submit to their fate. They have reached the point where there's no denying it. As St. Luke says in the third Gospel, "For nothing is hid that shall not be made manifest, nor anything secret that shall not be known and come to light." But Dante employs a poetic justice, known in the Italian as *contrapasso.* This is where the punishment is fitted to the vice each person yielded to while alive. One example is of those who loved flattering others with their tongues to gain preferential treatment; you know what that means. Now in Hell they must remain immersed in human excrement for all eternity. In short, if you liked sticking your nose in the 'brown stuff' while alive, for eternity you'll have all you want. But what was ultimately being *made known* to them? What exactly has *come to light* regarding this vice and all defects? Hopefully, that's obvious by this point. It's inherent in the title, *Ways of Love*. Every offense being punished in Hell is against *Love*, the ultimate theological virtue. They've lost their *Way of Love*.

So, now see all of your defects in terms of how they affect love. When the love you demonstrate with your life is simply not sufficient; that is the vice of *Sloth*. Or it may happen that you entirely miss or simply forget the fact that the object of your love must be God. Even as this love works through others in your world, or when God's beneficence is found in those necessary and good material things that are given to you in this life. In other words, when love never reaches or goes where it's intended, then it is the offense of *Lust, Greed* or *Gluttony*. Thirdly, out of weakness, it's easy to twist the concept of love. Love either gets disguised or seems to stop short at the secondary things or goods in your life. Love gets confused with earthly passions by those defects and appears as the vices of *Pride, Anger* or *Envy*.

To begin this theme, you will list some of your loving traits. It's certain you've not only become aware of your defects in the *Ways of Love*, but also how plentifully some loving traits appear in you. Then, you'll identify your worst defect and observe how it manifests itself in your life. Then you'll switch to the receiving end and observe it in other's lives. After that, you'll consider how this particular defect affects your life in *little* ways, and then how it manifests in those *big* ways. The theme will then proceed by your attempting to uncover what fear underlies this defect in you. That will take some time and reflection on your part. Then, in hopeful optimism, you will envision your life totally absent of that defect. In other words, you'll visualize what it will be like when that identifiable characteristic defect of yours is gone completely. You can do it, even if that liar Satan says it's impossible and causes you to doubt. The final reflection of the *Ways of Love* is a celebration. It's learning that although the Evil one lies, God's ways of love are immeasurably greater; in your life, He will win!

The final portion now of this theme introduction is really the preparation for the subsequent reflections. It's kept for last to remain first in your mind. You should spend the better part of an hour in prayer, even if you already know what your defect is. Do not overthink this prayer. Go in front of the Sacrament and just sit. Be quiet and listen. Or if you are unable to do that, find a place of solitude in your house or some other place where you can be alone. Enter this prayer with the foundations of humility and a contrite heart. St. Augustine remarked how in prayer, man is a beggar before God. Prayer is nothing more than the encounter of God's thirst with your hunger. Begin an internal dialogue with your Creator. Respond to the gift He has given you. In an act of adoration, acknowledge that you are a creature before your Creator, and just be silent. Ask and cry out with your soul that He may forgive you and then with your life, petition that the Kingdom of God may reign in you and the world. Ask the Saints to intercede on your behalf; you're all part of the same Mystical Body of Christ. In thanksgiving, recognize all the good things God has given and done for you. In your heart, praise the King of Kings who desires total union with you in love. Do those things!

If your faith supports it, visit with a Priest for the sacrament and mystery of confession. You have probably never prepared so wonderfully and fully before for reconciliation. Seek forgiveness for this defect and all the shock waves it has sent out in your life. You are so interconnected and interdependent; no fault is private.

Ask forgiveness also for the effects of that defect in those you love, and those you work with or go to school with, and in the community in which you live. There's no rush on this theme, so do not let anxiety slide in. Do not be concerned over progressing slowly, but be certain to complete these in an orderly and purposeful fashion. Just do so with patience and deep reflection. Allow God to finish the work He has begun in you and ask that now He brings it to completion. God bless you, and may His angels keep you! Amen!!!!

"I fled Him down the night and down the days...of my own mind, and in the midst of tears I hid from him."

Francis Thompson, *The Hound of Heaven*

It is not a question of whether the Hare or the Tortoise is quicker, but action and effort make the determination. In Aesop's famous "The Hare and the Tortoise," after the challenge was decided, each began the race as the Fox stood as judge. The Hare rapidly pulled ahead and thinking how silly it was for the Tortoise to even consider the contest, he laid down along the course to nap. Meanwhile, the Hare now sleeping was passed and awoke to only discover the Tortoise crossing the finish line—the race does not always favor the swift, but the persistent.

"According the modernity, it is morbid to confess your sins, I should say that the morbid thing is not to confess them. The morbid thing is to conceal your sins and let them eat your heart out, which is the happy state of most people in highly civilized communities."

G. K. Chesterton in *Daily News,* 1908

JOURNAL 92

LISTING MY LOVING TRAITS

"A good name is to be chosen rather than great riches" (Proverbs 12:1)

Things to consider: There is much good to be found in you! It is not being egotistical or to lack humility in recognizing that fact in yourself. You should know by this point in the *Ways of Love* that true humility is an honest self-assessment. If you're empathetic, and someone comments on how effortlessly you work with people who have disabilities, it's not humble to deny it or diminish your charism. You should thank them for recognizing the gift God gave you, and that you do your best to nurture its use for others; that's rightly ordered self-love. So, look back through the previous journal reflections to find 'answers' to the following prompts. What specifically have you learned new about yourself? Is there a characteristic that others always seemed to comment you possess? Do others often call you kind? Or tell you that you always seem to cooperate? Are you trustworthy, at least your friends always think so? And how about those virtues you read about in the introduction to this theme? Maybe you have some of those 'potential' virtues of meekness, kindness and such. Be creative; this is all preparation for further growth. So, for this reflection, you should list three loving traits you possess; first, identify a new one you've discovered, then a long-held one, and finally one you're determined to nurture more so as to increase in love. Take your time—this is God's time. Consider it!

266

MY CHALLENGE OF LISTING MY LOVING TRAITS

_____

_____

_____

_____

_____

_____

_____

_____

_____

_____

_____

_____

_____

_____

_____

_____

_____

_____

_____

_____

_____

_____

_____

_____

_____

Journal 93

Identifying My Worst Defect

"Do not be conformed to this world, be transformed by renewal" (Rom. 12:2)

Things to consider: "Be not afraid." Those were the words Karol Wojtyła pronounced three times as he addressed the throngs of people gathered in Vatican Square on October 22, 1978. They were gathered with their eyes on who might be this newly elected Pope; it was the former Bishop of Krakow in Poland. He said...

> Do not be afraid. Christ knows 'what is man'. He alone knows it. So often today man does not know what is within him, in the depths of his mind and heart. So often he is uncertain about the meaning of his life on this earth. He is assailed by doubt, a doubt which turns into despair. We ask you therefore, we beg you with humility and trust, let Christ speak to man. He alone has the words of life, yes, of eternal life.[33]

Now known as St. Pope John Paul II, this man knew the spiritual and psychological fear that grips you in your world. The fear he spoke of is not just some physiological response to your perceived dangers. This fear is much worse; it pertains to the existential questioning of purpose in a world that one cannot control. But just like psychological phobias, this fear must be identified and confronted. Read back through the theme introduction if you haven't yet ferreted out your worst defect. You may just write it down as a word or phrase, but feel free to add any background you think is important, and any hopes you have in overcoming it. The *hope* spoken of here is defined as a firm expectation in a future possible good. This hope is not for you to *change the world* by conquering your worst defect. That is not within your power. Your goal is transforming yourself in the world. Have courage and do not be afraid! Consider it!

MY CHALLENGE OF IDENTIFYING MY WORST DEFECT

_____

_____

_____

_____

_____

_____

_____

_____

_____

_____

_____

_____

_____

_____

_____

_____

_____

_____

_____

_____

_____

_____

_____

JOURNAL 94

OBSERVING MY DEFECT IN MYSELF

"But as for you, O man of God, shun all these things" (1 Tm. 6:11)

Things to consider: The best way to work through this reflection is to provide some examples of the defect in your life. Don't write yet of *how* it affects you, that's coming up. First, you need to know it will take a great deal of spiritual and emotional maturity to work through this reflection. As an analogy, the average person will notice a badly dented car door. But a specialist will point out a depression or scratch you didn't even know was there. It took a keen eye to look for shadows in the paint that revealed an almost imperceptible dent, and the scratch only became visible because it was seen in the proper lighting. You're more complex than an automobile, but with the scrutiny of searching in the 'shadows' of your actions and with the proper reflection of the Holy Spirit, your once unnoticed defects will soon appear obvious. So, for this journal, consider what triggers your defect. Think in terms of what you're doing when it happens. Ask maybe whom you are with when it occurs. What circumstances might be present? Is it when you are experiencing fatigue, irritation, anxiety, unexpected duties? Maybe it's when you are not at your best, or perhaps it's ironically when you are feeling quite comfortable that you let down your guard. How do you observe it in yourself? Consider it!

My Challenge of Observing Myself

JOURNAL 95

OBSERVING MY DEFECT IN OTHERS

"I do not pray that thou should take them out of the of the world" (John 17:15)

Things to consider: Though not *of* it, you are *part* of the world and in the world you must stay…God willing for a while yet anyway. You might want to be miles away from some people, sometimes, and you probably understand that some people share that sentiment of you. In reality, you like many people, and love a few. But that fact doesn't allow you to turn a blind eye to those annoying things you observe in those people you love. You can't help but recognize their personal defects, and you should probably notice you share a few. Isn't it much easier to notice your defects occurring in others? You're not being asked to be judgmental, but rather to use this observation as an opportunity for how your personal defect manifests itself in someone else. It can be a very enlightening experience and will certainly lead to a better understanding of how the same defect in you looks to others. So, you're going to have go down memory lane and see if you recall any instances of noticing _____ in others. When you saw it, what was your initial reaction? Did you think less of them? Did you think they were weak? Did it stir up indignation in your heart? Did you consider approaching them about this defect? How long was it until you realized it was a defect you both shared? Once you realized that, did you feel more sympathetic? Did you feel any less judgmental? Did it convict you? Consider it!

My Challenge of Observing Others

JOURNAL 96

LITTLE WAYS MY DEFECT AFFECTS MY LIFE

"He saved us, not because of deeds done by us in righteousness" (Titus 3:5a)

Things to consider: This reflection is not about how your defect affects you in big ways; that's next. This one is about those little consequences of your defect that sometimes never get connected to the root cause. For example, how does being a rude person sometimes rear its ugly head in one's life? First, consider the obvious. How might it affect those whom you love? Rudeness creates a barrier; people would choose to avoid a rude person rather than deal with the grumblings. If this were you, you might coincidently feel inferior because people don't confide in you. Or you might have a sense of isolation, as there would be a lack in camaraderie between you and your friends. And then think of the corrosive effect rudeness has as time passes. Slight differences in opinion could easily appear more pronounced, as rudeness is mistaken for disapproval. Over time, bitterness could fester and reduce trust. Friends would not ask favors of you fearing to deal with the rude attitude. Under this scenario, if you're the one who feels isolated, inferior, lacking camaraderie, finding yourself often misinterpreted or without close confidences, you may not realize it was *your* rudeness as the underlying cause. In what ways does your defect dismantle other healthy characteristics of support and love in your life? If some of your relationships appear frustrated, could your defect be the root cause? Consider it!

My Challenge of Little Ways it Affects My Life

JOURNAL 97

BIG WAYS MY DEFECT AFFECTS MY LIFE

"If I were pleasing men, I should not be a servant of Christ" (Gal. 1:10b)

Things to consider: Being impatient can ruin opportunities. If impatience were your defect, think of the impact it would have on your life in big ways. How would it affect your education? Cheaters are impatient; they prefer it to learning what method works for their schooling or putting in extra effort if they learn at a slower pace than others. Once out of college, impatience could even appear as indifference. Everyone knows it takes time to cultivate a career, so the impatient person may just step out of the search and take a position they are overqualified for because it was quicker and easier. Or it could work the other way, and they become brownnosers. Instead of putting in the hard effort and time so their quality work might be noticed, they might join the *right* clubs, eat at the *right* restaurants, etc., in order to be noticed...some even think that is exactly what people should do. Then concerning relationships, there's a certain truth to the notion that sexually active teens and those extra-marital affairs stem from impatience. Any time a quick pleasure is sought over a relationship that requires time for trust and genuine charity to develop, a lack of patience is present. In short, it might not be self-evident that struggles with fidelity in relationships, flattery, or demands for instant gratification are really rooted in lacking patience. Connect your defect to those 'big' areas of your life. Recognize the effect it has on you in ways unknown. Consider it!

MY CHALLENGE OF BIG WAYS IT AFFECTS MY LIFE

JOURNAL 98

WHAT FEAR UNDERLIES MY DEFECT?

"He who fears is not perfected in love" (1 Jn. 4:18b)

Things to consider: You are very good at rationalizing motives for your own character traits, especially concerning your now known defect. Here's a scenario: people who brownnose or cheat might say that they work and study hard, but others still seem to get ahead of them—so they justify their actions. It's thought they're just making the playing field even, adjusting for a handicap. Rude people who never seem to find a close-knit group of friends that they can trust or confide in, would probably transfer the blame to everyone else and in self-pity claim they're returning the ignorant behavior they've received. But once the brownnoser sees through their false justification and recognizes impatience as the culprit, they have to ask why? When the pity party is over, will the rude person realize what fear underlies their behavior? This is complex. It might be impatience stems from insecurity, i.e., the instant gratification is really a fear of not being competent or talented enough to reach their goals. Likewise, rudeness that results in a pity party could have at its foundation previous taunting where confrontations became a way of blocking ridicule, i.e., their rudeness is really a fear of being mocked. So, it might be the first person fears failing, and the second fears receiving ridicule. But wouldn't knowing that help? What fear is at the root of your defect? Think of your motive(s) and take time to really analyze it and distill it down similar to the above examples. Consider it!

MY CHALLENGE OF MY UNDERLYING FEAR

JOURNAL 99

VISION OF YOUR LIFE WITHOUT THE DEFECT

"You, therefore, must be perfect, as your heavenly Father is perfect" (Mt. 5:48)

Things to consider: In the "Suggested Approach" section, it was said 'three steps forward, two steps back' would be a description of how things will proceed in your *Ways of Love*. You know that's true. So, you've made some progress in this theme. Could you imagine what your life will be like when you conquer that defect? Just know that to conquer it means you took three steps forward. Do not think that when you experience those two steps back, your journey was a failure. As you continue on with the *Ways of Love*, it won't be long before you once again go three steps forward. At that point, recognize you're going in the right direction. Your progress is incremental. It's always that way with difficult growth, so keep that in mind. With that underlying fear removed, gone will be how that defect affects your life in those little and big ways. Shedding that fear is large part of the victory. One last thing, it's intimidating to think of *never* doing it again. Consider this: when a person tries to quit smoking, it's a daunting proposal. Like smoking, there's an addictive quality to the defect in your life, and the thought of *never* doing it again can seem overwhelming. But the urge to smoke is not constant, and that temptation only lasts for a short while. So, a smoker really only needs to quit for a *short while* until he or she has established the new habit. Do the same thing with your defect. Don't *quit* forever, but only when the conditions reappear. For this reflection, be creative describing how your life will be different without that defect. Consider it!

MY CHALLENGE OF ENVISIONING MYSELF

JOURNAL 100

THE SPIRITUAL MARATHON IS OVER, FOR NOW

"I press on to make it my own, [for] Christ has made me his own" (Phil. 3:12b)

Things to consider: The *Way of Love* is over for *now*; it's a new beginning. Sound cliché? But it's a reality. It's a growth process, and one you will (should) go through at least a few times throughout your life. You spent a considerable amount of time and energy, so keep this journal as a snapshot of who you *were* now. Look back at this *picture* in the upcoming years. How much more will this reveal than an actual photo? It's captured your depth, reflected your challenges, and recorded your insights. There's nothing two-dimensional about *this* picture of you. Now, there is still something for you to write for this 100th journal. It's an opportunity to critique your 'performance'. Not in terms *good* or *bad*, but to make some quick notes to improve your approach for the next opportunity. You know of the times you've planned something out and found as soon as it was over that you had a few good ideas on how to make it better. Not writing those down meant you had to rely on your memory when the next event arrived. Do it now while it is fresh in your head. Don't hesitate to consider tweaking the focus of some prompts to fit your personality or particular approach. There are multiple ways to direct some of the reflection considerations. The *Ways of Love* is intended to allow the Spirit to work through *you*! Make your notes now. Always know God loves you, so now go love others! Consider it!

My Reflections on My Spiritual Marathon

_____

_____

_____

_____

_____

_____

_____

_____

_____

_____

_____

_____

_____

_____

_____

_____

_____

_____

_____

_____

_____

_____

_____

_____

_____

EPILOGUE

FINAL CONSIDERATIONS

There is an expected experience that eating healthy for 100 days does not undo years of bad dietary habits. Too, exercising regularly and well for a few months cannot immediately overcome the effects of a previously sedentary lifestyle. But each of those is a beginning; a setting oneself on the right path to break the habit of neglect where comfort was chosen over health. The problem is that despair and apathy set in quickly when we do not perceive our efforts as demonstrating the effect noticeably, and before you know it, we're back to eating poorly and laying around. The truth is that it takes time to see future benefits, but it also takes more than to simply 'know' that simple fact.

You should expect nothing different in what you have just completed. Re-creating one's character—moving from vice to virtue—requires first a reorientation, and then perseverance. Any person who has broken an addiction knows that good habits need to supersede bad habits, and then one must 'stick with it' especially when a new comfort level is attained. And as important as your feelings are, they are not good indicators of what is genuinely good for you—if you're not careful, temporal feelings tend to seek pleasure, and we are very good at rationalizing our actions.

Spiritual growth is incremental and must be maneuvered around life's various preoccupations, physical and mental fatigue, and indifference, and one should not be ashamed to also admit levels of ignorance. The reality is that like most things, it is not a matter of intellectually understanding what is a genuinely good for us as a person which leads to transformation. Every person who smokes recognizing the health risks; he or she didn't start smoking to increase those risks, so simply recognizing the potential harm is not sufficient knowledge to quit. At some moment, whatever is harmful as a vice is not overcome until we realize that doing 'it' brings us more pain than pleasure. These 'recognized moments' are discoveries that we must seize—they are moments of grace.

This applies to most all things 'learned in the heart'. There are those truths which were previously known (or knowable) intellectually, but never found their way as moments of action into our lives. The interesting fact, though, is that once discovered, these truths about us, others, and our world *cannot* be unknown. They become part of our personal wisdom; an aspect of 'who' we are and have become. And just like eating right and exercising both contribute to our physical health, this 'self-knowledge' adds to our experiential personal character and will have benefits that cannot quite be quantified. Think of how you would feel if someone acknowledges your weight loss or tells you that you look in shape. If exercise and diet can over the course of spans of time allow others to see *the* change, ever more so will your continued character development become apparent to those in your life and world—and ultimately to yourself.

But in case you begin to think this is simply about you, be clear that this *transformed* you is not intended as an end in itself…it is not simply about self-change. Through your own transformation, you can and will transform the world in ways no political policy or social system could ever have the power to accomplish. You never had the power for that anyway, but you have one-hundred percent control of who you are, and your spiritual relation with God, others, and all creation. Until the next round…

May God's peace be with your transformed self until you return to the Love Incarnate with whose Being you are in harmony and who sustains you in existence.

ENDNOTES

[1] See Alexander Solzhenitsyn, "The Exhausted West," *Harvard Magazine*, July-August (1978), 21-6.

[2] See G. K. Chesterton, *What's Wrong With the World* (San Francisco: Ignatius Press, 1910), 17.

[3] Chesterton, 53.

[4] See Chesterton, 53.

[5] For a fuller discussion, see Aristotle, *The Nicomachean Ethics*, trans. Harris Rackham (Hertfordshire, England: Wordsworth Editions Limited, 1996), 36-7.

[6] For a fuller treatment of Shelton's gratitude inventory, see Charles M. Shelton, *The Gratitude Factor: Enhancing Your Life Through Grateful Living* (Mahwah, NJ: Hidden Spring, 2010), 22-6.

[7] Found in Alexander Pope's *An Essay on Criticism* (Hard Press Publishing: 2010).

[8] You can read a fuller explanation of C. S. Lewis' handling of this notion in the first chapter of *The Abolition of Man* (NY, New York: Harper One, 2000) entitled "Men Without Chests."

[9] This line was the quote of a prince, who was reportedly in love. It can be found in Fyodor Dostoevsky, *The Idiot* (NY, New York: The Modern Library, 2003), 415.

[10] For a more detailed description of Aristotle's types of friendships, see Book Eight of *The Nicomachean Ethics*, particularly pages 207-09.

[11] Pope Pius XI, Encyclical on Reconstruction of the Social Order *Quadragesimo anno* (15 May 1931), §50, at The Holy See, w2.vatican.va.

[12] St. Benedict wrote, "Hospitality maintains a prominence in the living (Christian) tradition [because] the guest represents Christ and has a claim on the welcome and care of the community." St. Benedict, *The Rule of Saint Benedict*, Anthony C. Meisel and M. L. del Mastro (trans), (New York, NY: Image Books Doubleday). See specifically Chapter LIII, "The Reception of Guests," 89-90.

[13] You may find more on hospitality and the home in *Living the Hospitality of God* by Fr. Lucien Richard, O.M.I. (Mahwah, NJ: Paulist Press, 2000). See particularly the section entitled "Hospitality to the Stanger: Putting It in Perspective" on pages 5-13.

[14] It has been reported that the Emperor Napoleon once vowed he would destroy the Church. Pope Pius VII replied, "We the clergy have been trying to do so for 1800 years. We have not succeeded, and neither will you."

[15] Fr. Thomas Dubay, S.M., *Prayer Primer: A Fire Within*, (San Francisco, CA: Ignatius Press, 2002). Dubay points out that this longing of communicating for the infinite is unique to humans. If you personally experience difficulty in your prayer life, it will behoove you to see Chapter 15, "Problems and Pitfalls," 147-56.

[16] For Martin Buber, all *encounters* whether they are a language exchange or communication through silence, are essential for growth and development. See Martin Buber, *I and Thou*, Walter Kaufmann (trans), (New York, NY: Simon & Schuster, 1996), 53-85.

[17] Brendan Byrne, S.J., in his commentary on that passage in the *Sacra Pagina* series points out that it ultimately means no government (or any person) is a 'law unto themselves', but rather all authority is ultimately answerable to God. For a fuller explanation, see Brendan Byrne, *Sacra Pagina*, "Romans," v6,

Daniel J. Harrington (ed), (Collegeville, MN: The Liturgical Press, 1996), 387-88.

[18] Aesop, *Aesop's Fables*, (New York, NY: Barnes & Noble, 2012), "The Owls, the Bats, and the Sun," 151.

[19] The Seven Deadly Vices are thought to have found their origins in the latter part of the 4th century with St. Evagrius Ponticus, and bought to the Latin West by St. John Cassian. Some of his insights from his *Remedies for the Eight Principal Faults* will be incorporated into the descriptions. The list and brief commentary presented here is only intended to be a synopsis. The list order will follow Pope Gregory I's canon as accepted by St. Thomas Aquinas in his *Summa theologica*.

[20] See the Epistle of James 1:17. It follows his promise of be blessed for enduring trials and standing the test. That person will receive the crown of life promised to whose God loves.

[21] Thomas Aquinas, *Summa theologiae*, II-II, q153, a3, co., in *Summa theologica*: Complete English Edition in Five Volumes, vol. IV, trans. Fathers of the English Dominican Provence (Westminister, MD: Christian Classics, 1911), 1806.

[22] John Cassian, *The Twelve Books on the Institutes of the Coenobia and the Remedies of the Eight Principal Faults*, Edgar C. S. Gibson (trans), (Aeterna Press, 2015), 71. See Book V, Chapter XVII entitled, "That the Foundation and Basis of the Spiritual Combat Must Be Laid in the Struggle Against Gluttony."

[23] Thomas Aquinas, vol. III, ST, II-II, q118, a1, co., 1680.

[24] Cassian, 89. See Book VII, Chapter II entitled, "How Dangerous is the Disease of Covetousness."

[25] Cassian, 127. See Book X, Chapter VI entitled, "How Injurious Are the Effects of Accidie."

[26] Thomas Aquinas, vol. III, ST, II-II, q35, a1, co., 1339.

[27] Cassian, 106. See Book VIII, Chapter I entitled, "How Our Fourth Conflict is Against the Sin of Anger, and How Many Evils This Passion Produces."

[28] Thomas Aquinas, vol. IV, ST, II-II, q158, a7, 1837.

[29] Thomas Aquinas, vol. III, ST, II-II, q36, a1, ad.2, 1343.

[30] Thomas Aquinas, vol. IV, ST, II-II, q1162, a2, co., 1849.

[31] John Milton, *Paradise Lost* (New York, NY: Modern Library, 2008), line 263, p. 24

[32] Cassian, 162. See Book XII, Chapter XXXIII entitled, "Remedies Against the Evil of Pride."

[33] Pope John Paul II, Homily of His Holiness John Paul II For the Inauguration of His Pontificate, §5, St. Peter's Square (22 October 1978), at The Holy See, w2.vatican.va.